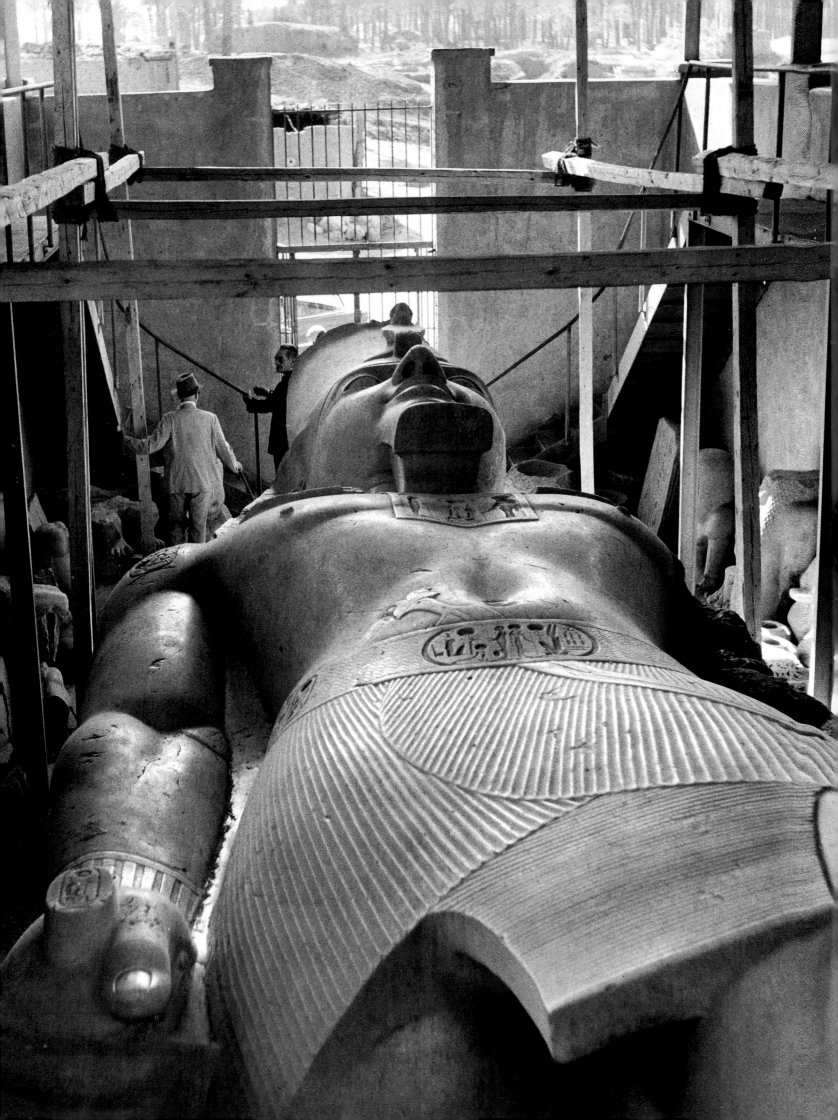

PRODUCED & DESIGNED BY JOHN LYNCH · INTRODUCTION BY GEORGE EELLS

Travels
WITH
COLE
PORTER

TEXT &
PHOTOGRAPHS BY
Jean
HOWARD

HARRY N. ABRAMS, INC., PUBLISHERS, NEW YORK

EDITOR: Harriet Whelchel

UP FRONT:

Endsheets: Cole Porter in the comfort of his Caddie as the ferry makes its way from Messina to Cosenza, April 5, 1956.

   A few of the notes I received from Cole over the years—he could say more in a line than most people could in a book.

Page 1: Linda Porter photographed by Edward Steichen, 1926.

Pages 2 and 3: Memphis, Egypt, 1956. Cole (upper left), in the shed surrounding the recumbent statue of Ramses II, approaching Paul Sylvain for help in mounting the stairs to the viewing gallery above.

   Howard Sturges, Cole, and Linda viewing the same statue on their 1921 cruise up the Nile.

Pages 6 and 7: Cole on the deck of the *Eros II* as we arrive in the harbor at Mykonos, Greece, 1955.

   Two of the *Eros II* crew waiting to take us ashore, Greek islands, 1955.

Library of Congress Cataloging-in-Publication Data

Howard, Jean.
   Travels with Cole Porter/photographs by Jean Howard:
   introduction by George Eells; design by John Lynch.
      p.   cm.
   Includes index.
   ISBN 0–8109–3408–6 (cloth)
      1. Porter, Cole, 1891–1964—Journeys. 2. Composers—
   United States—Biography. I. Title.
   ML410.P7844H7 1991
   782.1'4'092'—dc20
   [B]   91–10519
                                                                        CIP

Published in 1991 by Harry N. Abrams, Incorporated, New York
A Times Mirror Company

Printed and bound in Japan

acknowledgments

My deepest thanks go to the following people:

Stuart E. Jacobson, who from the moment he saw my photographs visualized books and made them happen. Stuart, you are missed and loved.

Robert A. Montgomery, Jr., attorney and trustee of the Cole Porter Musical and Literary Trusts, for his encouragement and help throughout this undertaking.

Florence Leeds, executive secretary of the Porter Trusts, for her understanding and help in organizing essential facts for our book.

Richard Warren, Jr., curator of the Historical Sound and Recordings Department at the Yale University Library, for his help in locating archival photographs and checking factual information for the book.

Paul Gottlieb, president of Harry N. Abrams, Inc., for his quiet strength in publishing only the best in books.

Glenn Bernbaum, an original, and my greatest booster, who turned his restaurant, Mortimer's, into an exciting picture gallery for *Jean Howard's Hollywood* and gave a great party.

Camilla McGrath, a fine photographer herself, for her pictures of her mother, Contessa Pecci Blunt, and of Cole's "beloved Gabriella," Principessa Gardinelli—and for helping to identify the girls in the 1956 party picture in St. Moritz. Thanks, Camilla; you're a pal.

Leo Lerman, for his applause and encouragement through the years—deepest thanks.

Tony Santoro, steady and reliable. As always, my love.

Billy McCarty Cooper, a special friend, for his interest and suggestions for this book, and for the grandest party ever for *Jean Howard's Hollywood*. Deepest thanks, Billy.

George Eells, a friend through the years. Your help has been tremendous throughout this endeavor—my thanks.

Harriet Whelchel, my long-distance editor. So happy you are here on this one—a million thanks.

Michael Pearman. It was the Porters who introduced us—and you've held my hand ever since. With love.

Marti Stevens, without whose companionship a lot of this book simply would not have happened. With love.

Liz Robbins and her group of P.R. people at Harry N. Abrams, Inc., all so bright and with it—a million thanks.

Harriet Blacker, who brings a lot of class to the world of public relations. You are the top.

PUBLISHER'S NOTE: The letters of Cole and Linda Porter and the travel diaries of Cole Porter (in *italic* type, signed CP) are reproduced in their entirety. Jean Howard's travel diary (in *italic* type, signed JH) has been altered slightly for reasons of continuity and to avoid duplication of material, and the author has provided additional explanatory captions. Idiosyncrasies of spelling and style established by the earlier sources are carried forth throughout the book, with bracketed explications given where deemed necessary.

CONTENTS

INTRODUCTION
BY GEORGE EELLS 8

A PERFECT BLENDSHIP
10

INTRODUCTION

BY GEORGE EELLS

I WAS NEVER LUCKY ENOUGH to travel with Cole Porter—or the great Jean Howard, for that matter—unless you count frequent long drives to Cole's country place in Williamstown, Massachusetts. This is not stretching the point as far as one might think. Even an ordinary evening on the town was as meticulously planned by Cole as a journey to some exotic land.

Battling boredom as he grew older, he planned evenings weeks ahead and filled each with activity of one kind or another. On an ordinary night, if you were the only guest, Cole requested you be in the lobby of the Waldorf Towers at 8:15. Precisely on the dot, his smiling face, set above a well-cut suit with an ever-present untrimmed carnation in the lapel, would emerge from the elevator. After greetings, we would proceed to the waiting Cadillac town car to be driven to Le Pavillon (or the Colony or L'Aiglon), arriving on the tick of 8:20, dining and leaving the restaurant at 9:40 for a 10:01 showing of a new film at the Roxy (or the Paramount or Loews State). Afterward it was back to the Waldorf and Apartment 33-A, where he had a Cutty Sark and soda, and, unless you were strong willed, you ended up with a split of champagne, which Cole had taken a hate against but which well-meaning acquaintances still inundated him with at Christmas.

Frequently, the schedule was changed to include a surprise in the form of bonus guests. It might be Bea Lillie, who talked about the past; or Ethel Merman, who talked and talked about her latest triumphs; or Elsa Maxwell, who talked and talked and talked about her guest shots on the Jack Paar television show; or the Duc di Verdura, who gossiped about historical personages as if they were contemporaries; or Natasha Wilson, née Princess Paley, who once memorably evoked prerevolutionary Russia when her family traveled by private train past angry peasants to the Winter Palace. But the nicest, most interesting surprise was a tall, breathtaking champagne blond who turned out to be Jean Howard.

Cole was inordinately fond of Jean. In a typical Porterian ploy, he manufactured a titillative background, informing me that she had hitchhiked directly from Dallas, Texas, to New York, where she had immediately been chosen as a featured show girl in the *Ziegfeld Follies*.

Cole told not only me that story but also many other friends—and we all believed him. Only years later, when Jean happened to show me a photograph of herself as a Goldwyn girl in the film version of Eddie Cantor's *Whoopee!*, prior to her *Follies* stint, did I report the hoax our mutual friend had perpetrated. She roared with laughter. "That," said Jean, "is why Linda used to say Cole was an elf."

Actually I think Cole was so taken with Jean because in many ways she reminded him of a young Linda. She imparted a hint of mystery, an air of distinction—and she was great fun. Most of all, she was always on what is now called the cutting edge.

I remember commenting on this to Cole one evening in 1959 after Jean had urged me to get down to The Living Theater on Fourteenth Street to see a play, still in previews, called *The Connection*. As entertainment editor of *Look* magazine, I was aware of the undertaking, but this scruffy, avant-garde troupe

doing a play about drug addiction was hardly the fare you expected to be touted in Cole's luxurious apartment. Afterward I mentioned my surprise to Cole, who responded, "That's the great Jean. She's always onto things before anyone else."

Over the years I've known her, she has continued to develop—which is probably why after all these years she has begun bringing out books filled with her wonderful photographs.

Although I never took a long trip with Cole, actually I experienced many of his trips by proxy. In later years, I frequently received what he said were the longest letters he had ever written, describing in detail his small adventures.

Despite his insistence that he had no aptitude for writing prose, those letters convinced me that had he not chosen to become a songwriter he could have written classic travel books. The letters recounted his delight in roaming the world to satisfy his insatiable curiosity about all the conventional and unconventional sights and sounds and experiences both thrilling and boring ("It's just as much fun hating something as liking it," he used to maintain).

This voracious appetite to *see* may sometimes have been wearying on his traveling companions, but it provided grist for interesting correspondence as he utilized his painterly eye to describe scenic beauty and historic sites on the one hand and a simple luncheon at a roadside taverna on the other. Cole was blessed with a keen sense of the incongruous, which in the Greek islands led him to cultivate the acquaintance of a former top whore who became her town's top bootblack, and in Egypt an old Arab who cried out, as Cole and his party were admiring the pyramids by moonlight, "Isn't it fantastic!" Eager to elicit special information, Cole attempted to engage the fellow in conversation. But those three words turned out to be the Arab's entire English vocabulary, learned from hearing over and over the not-so-original responses to the sight by thousands of American tourists.

When Cole was at his Waldorf Towers apartment, he enjoyed having his chauffeur, Bentley, take him on long drives to various parts of the five boroughs. I often accompanied him, and on these drives he frequently reminisced about, among other things, his earlier travels. Once he told me that his appetite for travel had been whetted as a small boy entranced by the polychromatic curtain depicting the Grand Canal that graced the proscenium arch of the Emric Theatre in his hometown of Peru, Indiana.

His love of travel definitely had been stimulated by his first trip abroad, a prep-school-graduation present, which allowed him to live with an ordinary French family for part of the summer, then travel through the countryside into Switzerland and Germany.

Even as a young man, Cole seems to have had a knack for seeking out the best. His friend Abe Burrows once remarked that he had known many people who through luck, talent, beauty, shrewdness, or ruthlessness had managed to accumulate fortunes greater than Cole's, but not a single one of them who knew as well how to enjoy the things money can buy. Cole put it another way. "There was always enough money—never enough beauty," he said —so he went searching for it.

Whatever was beautiful, esoteric, or just out of the ordinary provided a lifelong fascination. Once he planned a jaunt from Hollywood to New York by way of Calander, Ontario, to see the famed Dionne quintuplets. In Europe he detoured hundreds of miles on one trip to view a herd of reindeer. He sent descriptions home of "a chic little Greek church" and went to Cuba to bake his legs in the sun after he'd injured them in a riding accident. He also took in Havana's hot spots. Asked his opinion of the city, he mischievously said, "Heaven must be awfully like Havana."

Linda, Cole's wife, was as tireless about absorbing and understanding the remains of previous cultures as he. When things became tiresome in one place, the Porters simply gathered a group of friends, engaged a private railroad car or hopped a boat, and set out on a new adventure. Their attitudes are reflected in this postcard sent when Cole revisited one of those places after Linda's death. "Sicily is a dream," he wrote, "that I remember so well when Linda and I honeymooned here years ago. And this Palermo has so many beautiful examples of so many civilizations that one could see and see for months."

But his approach was not always so elevated. In 1930 after the opening in rapid succession of *Fifty Million Frenchmen* and *Wake Up and Dream*, the Porters and Mrs. "Dumpy" Oelrichs, a fun-loving, gravel-voiced society woman, set out for Venice by way of Hollywood, China, and Japan. From Hawaii, the Malay Straits, Nangpo Colony, and Siam, the songwriter who claimed he cared nothing for publicity wrote a song "inspired" by each locale and sent them back to the United States for possible inclusion in *Fifty Million Frenchmen* and definitely to help promote the show.

Once, in an excess of high spirits while visiting Japan at the height of the Depression, Cole became testy about mediocre train service and attracted unfavorable headlines by leasing an entire train to transport his small party and their servants. He was about to blunder again when upon encountering Clyde Beatty in Ceylon, he proposed as a practical joke buying a baby elephant and having animal trainer Beatty deposit it on the Porters' friend Monty Woolley's doorstep. Linda's saner judgment prevailed, and additional headlines critical of their hedonistic life-style were averted.

The trip Cole recalled most fondly, however, was the world tour he and Moss Hart decided to take when they agreed to work together on *Jubilee*. In January of 1935, with Linda, Howard Sturges, Monty Woolley, and travel writer Bill Powell in tow, Cole and Hart set off on the Cunard White Star liner *Franconia*. Included in Cole's voluminous luggage were a small metronome, a typewriter, a small piano organ, two dozen black pencils, a quire of music paper, recordings of *Anything Goes*, a phonograph, and three cases of Grand Chambertin '87. At a press conference, Cole observed: "Most of the music in that part of the world [Tahiti, Samoa, Bali] is played from memory. If I can write it down fast enough, I may get another 'Night And Day' out of it."

Cole's ability to concentrate aroused envy in Hart as he observed Cole writing songs on the sun deck of the ship, flying over Africa, climbing Indian ruins, and "never once, come weal or woe, [allowing] it to interfere with his personal life."

Just as Cole delighted in offering surprises during evenings in Manhattan, he also enjoyed arranging them on trips. During the *Jubilee* tour, for instance, Linda let drop that she had always longed for an audience with the sultan of Zanzibar, which she understood to be impossible. Days later, Cole handed her a cable reading: "ADVISE CRUISE DIRECTOR, FRANCONIA, AUDIENCE SULTAN ARRANGED FOR COLE PORTER PARTY."

At 10:30 A.M. on the appointed day, the men and Linda boarded the royal launch. After entering the palace, they had their topees taken by a robed attendant before climbing a solid-ebony staircase to the throne room. The sultan, who was in the midst of a three-day fast, served the Porter party a local delicacy (sherbet), inquired about his friends Lady Cunard and Alfred Duff Cooper (who had arranged the meeting), and displayed a Ping-Pong set, a recent gift from Lady Cunard. "He seemed disappointed that none of us challenged him to a game," Cole later maintained as evidence that the sultan was bored to distraction. The whole adventure—including the tinge of absurdity in the pseudo pomp—was of a type Cole would remember always. Strangely, no reference to it crept into his lyrics.

Lesser events did inspire hit songs. In the 1935 trip around the world, Cole said he had heard so much about the glorious sunrise over the Rio Harbor that he and Linda arose early to go on deck to witness it. There they encountered Monty Wooley, who had spent the night lifting a few. As Cole told it, when dawn broke he exclaimed, "It's delightful."

Linda added, "It's delicious."

And tipsy Monty chimed in, "It's de-lovely."

The resultant song, which went into *Red, Hot and Blue*, even won acclaim from the usually taciturn G-Man J. Edgar Hoover, who as a first-nighter modestly acknowledged he knew a hit when he heard one.

I've always thought that of all his trips—including the two fascinating ones Jean photographed—the one that gave the truest measure of Cole as a human being occurred in 1939, two years after the accident in which a horse he was riding fell and crushed both of his legs, leaving him in constant pain. Nevertheless, with his doctors' blessings, Cole set out with his friend Ray Kelly and his valet Paul Sylvain for Machu Picchu in Peru.

On the last lap of the journey, with his legs in braces, Cole was lifted to the back of a horse and negotiated the dusty mountain paths with sheer drops on either side that could have made a misstep by the mare fatal. Both Ray and Paul became apprehensive and urged turning back, but Cole was determined to explore the ruins. Once they had reached their destination, this sometimes demanding man, who frequently sent his daiquiri back two or three times because it was too sweet or too sour, uncomplainingly put up with the most primitive bathing and toilet facilities. And each morning, although still on canes, he persisted in going "slowly and in [his] own way" through the ruins so that before departing he had mastered the history and significance of what he had viewed.

I don't mean to give the impression Cole spoke only of his trips during our drives around the city: He filled me in on his family background, show-business gossip, and scandal of all kinds. Yet there was a great deal of emphasis on travel. I began to understand its importance to him only after his death, when another friend of his, Sam Stark, said Cole claimed that frittering away time made him uneasy. Travel, he told Stark, made him feel justified in turning out only an occasional song. Stark showed me a card written when work was not forthcoming. "This work, this job, this contract does not arrive and until it does, picture me as basically bored," Cole wrote. "Isn't it tragic to lose the power of enjoying doing nothing? I am surrounded by all the creature comforts and major amusements, but it is not enough."

Obviously his travels alleviated that guilt. Luckily for us, through Jean Howard's magical use of the camera, combined with the diaries that both she and Cole kept and the letters he wrote her, we get a clear picture not only of his final two trips but also of the man himself.

a Perfect Blendship

White STUDIO
ROUGH PROOF

THIS STORY REALLY BEGINS with a group of American expatriates living in Paris during World War I. It was in Paris, on January 13, 1918, that Ethel Borden Harriman married Henry Russell. At the reception that followed at the Ritz Hotel, Cole Albert Porter first met Linda Lee Thomas.

Cole was the twenty-seven-year-old only child from a wealthy Peru, Indiana, family, an aspiring composer in Paris broadening himself while enrolled at the Schola Cantorum to study musical composition. Linda was a sophisticated divorcée originally from Louisville, Kentucky. Considered by many the most beautiful woman in the world, she traveled with the elite of international society. She was eight years Cole's senior. On December 18 of the following year, she and Cole were married.

Linda brought Cole into the rich, glittering world that would hold an irresistible fascination for him most of his life. It fit him like a glove. If not for Linda, I don't know if he would have known that world—certainly not on the same level of sophistication. She stood strong by his side, guiding him through the lights and shadows of that world. Long before anyone else, Linda realized that Cole's talent amounted to genius, and she made him realize the importance of his work.

By 1931 Ethel Harriman Russell had landed in the *Ziegfeld Follies* via her rich and social friends' living rooms, where she used to have them rolling on the floor with laughter at her imitations. She could do Texas Guinan and Fanny Brice to a "T," but to her dismay and disappointment (mostly due to stage fright), she could not reach the audience at the Ziegfeld Theatre—and so her career as an actress didn't last very long.

It lasted long enough, however, for her to make a few new friends. Marie Stevens, one or two others, and I (I appeared in the last two *Follies* as a "special" show girl) were all attracted to her warm and outgoing personality. Actually, she played quite a part in my first years in Hollywood (but that's another story) and was a witness at my wedding to Hollywood agent Charles Feldman in 1934.

It was at one of Ethel's after-theater parties that I met Cole and Linda Porter. We liked each other instantly. I suppose I was a rather pretty girl with a definite Texas accent. I had always thought of myself as sophisticated but never a "socialite," yet the press got it into their heads that I was just *that*, and every society column from *then on* had me tagged as "a society girl"—from "the East, the West"—they didn't much care *where* as long as I looked the part. All this amused the Porters enormously. In any case, they sort of took me in and had me around quite a bit, inviting me to all their parties, where I met Noël Coward, Fanny Brice, Clifton Webb, Gertrude Lawrence, Elsa Maxwell, and countless other luminaries of the day.

The Porters came to Hollywood in December 1935. Cole had been contracted to write the score for an as-yet untitled MGM movie, which would turn out to be *Born to Dance*, starring Eleanor Powell and Jimmy Stewart, who was cast at Cole's suggestion. They rented the Richard Barthelmess house on Sunset Boulevard, a few blocks from where I lived with Charlie. Cole loved every moment of it; he once commented, "Hollywood, it's rather like living on the moon, isn't it?" Not so Linda. Cole had his work—he was always happiest when working. Linda loved gardening, but not in someone else's garden. Even with visits from friends like Howard Sturges, Dr. Albert Sirmay (Cole's music editor), R. C. Kelly, columnist Winsor French, Roger Stearns, and Baron Nicholas de Gunzberg, the days were long for her. She was no more enthusiastic about Hollywood nightlife. At the Porters' dinner parties for eight to ten guests, the conversation inevitably turned to business, which Linda found

Opposite: *Florenz Ziegfeld arranged to have
all his show girls make a trip to the White Studio for
publicity pictures. Here is a rough proof of one of mine,
taken in 1931, the year I met the Porters.*

Suddenly...They Wanted to Marry; They Did...Suddenly

Above, is the finish of a Modern Drama. Scene: Harrison, N. Y. Time: 1 A. M. Cast, l to r: Walter Wanger, friend; Charles K. Feldman, the groom; Jean Howard, the bride (with blush); and Ethel Borden Harriman, witness. Feldman married the famous MGM star in Harrison Friday night after discovering that to wed in Greenwich, Conn., require d a five-day application.

Above, clockwise from top left: *A newspaper
clipping of my wedding. Charlie and I are in the center, with
our witnesses, Walter Wanger and Ethel Harriman, left and right.
Cole before the fireplace at the Richard Barthelmess
house in Beverly Hills, 1936.
Bill Powell, Monty Woolley, Cole, Linda, and Howard Sturges
in Hawaii, on their 1935 cruise.*

boring and out of place at a social gathering. Then there were the evenings when Louella Parsons's husband, Dockie Martin, had one too many martinis and upped on the sofa, and Clark Gable, in an effort to be amusing, removed his upper bridge at the dinner table. The talk at table often became more than colorful, which annoyed her. Linda once commented to a guest, "My dear, I've heard all those words before. I've even done most of them, but I'd prefer not to dine on them."

Whatever their individual opinions, the Porters had a great deal to do with brushing Hollywood up on its social graces. For instance, most of us were accustomed to arriving at parties at 8 o'clock and never getting near the dinner table before 10. Naturally, we would be pretty well looped by then. Well, the Porters put an end to that. You were invited for 8:15, had time for two drinks, and were served dinner on the dot of 8:45. If you were late getting there—too bad. At 8:45 you sat down. Even after Linda's death, Cole continued in this disciplined attitude toward mealtimes, as I came to discover during our travels.

The Porters returned to Hollywood, and the Barthelmess house, the following summer (1937) for Cole's work on *Rosalie*. Linda, realizing Cole's love for Southern California, went so far as to look at several estates to purchase. Eventually the effect of the climate on her health made it obvious that she would never be able to live on the West Coast for any extended length of time, and plans to buy or

build a permanent residence were dropped. A few years later Cole would rent from Billy Haines, a silent-film-star-turned-decorator, a house at 416 Rockingham Drive in Brentwood, which he kept.

The first great turning point in Cole's life had been meeting Linda. The second occurred later in 1937 and was as devastating as the first had been fortunate. Cole, the Duc di Verdura, and others were weekend guests of Contessa Edith ("Tookie") de Zappola at Oyster Bay on Long Island. A riding party was organized at the Piping Rock Club in Locust Valley, and Cole suffered the freak riding accident that would result in almost constant pain for the rest of his life.

I absolutely adored Linda Porter. She had without a doubt the loveliest taste of anyone I have ever known. Her clothes were perfect; her Paris house, and later her apartment at the Waldorf Towers in New York, were ideal. I believe the Porters had a great deal to do with making the Waldorf Towers fashionable, as indeed they made everything they did fashionable. Her last home, called Buxton Hill, in Williamstown, Massachusetts, was the most beautiful of all.

I used to spend a few weeks every summer with Linda at Buxton Hill. Cole was mostly in California during the summers working on a new movie or for no other reason than he truly did love California.

Right: *I took these pictures of Cole and Sturges, around 1950, near the pool house at Cole's place in Brentwood. Originally Linda's friend, Sturges became very close with Cole and remained so. I am particularly fond of the straw-hat pictures — Cole always said, "I'm just a country boy from Peru, Indiana." At heart, he remained just that.*

Linda had Billy Baldwin update the caretaker's cottage for Cole. Knowing Cole as she did, she realized early in their first years of marriage that Cole would have to have his own living quarters and independence, and so from the beginning they had separate apartments. Now, in Williamstown, Cole had his own "house," where he was free to work any hour of the day or night and leave Linda undisturbed in her daily routine. He would come up to the "big" house for lunch and dinner and where Linda always had one or two charming houseguests—Howard Sturges and the designer Mainbocher, among others, were frequent guests.

Howard Sturges, a lifelong friend of the Porters', often stayed for weeks at a time. Sturges, or "Sturge," as he was often called, was independently wealthy and unconstrained by business schedules, although he was noted for his work with relief organizations both in the United States and France, where he had spent a great deal of time. At one time he had had a problem with alcohol, which Linda helped him to overcome. As was typical of Sturges, he later said to Linda, "I drank my way through two fortunes; luckily, I had a third."

The better you know some people, and the more you care for them, the harder it is to feel that you are presenting their personalities in the truest possible light. With this in mind, I have decided to let Linda and Cole speak for themselves—as they did to me—by including some of the letters I received from them over the years.

Left, above and below: *At a party to celebrate the unveiling of Paul Clemens's portrait of Anita Colby, at her Brentwood house, 1946. Anita and her portrait are at center; her guests included (left to right) Dusty Negulesco, Skitch Henderson, Quique and Louis Jourdan, Jean Negulesco, and Cole.*
Cole and Merle Oberon at a party in my living room in the mid-1950s. It was Merle who gave Cole his beloved little dog Peppi (aka Pep or Pepin le Bref IV).

THE WALDORF-ASTORIA
NEW YORK

Sunday [1938]

Dearest Jean:

Are you and Charlie floating about on a raft, and are you safe? The reports of the flood are horrible—*what* a disaster!

I meant to leave last Sunday for Tucson, but my plans were all changed as Coley went to the Doctor's Hospital for an examination and I wanted to hear results. He is doing splendidly, so that I leave next Wednesday to join Sturges at Triangle T Ranch, *Dragoon* Arizona, for three or four weeks. Sturges, who phoned me this morning, says it is simply divine——cooler air—4000 ft. high—perfectly quiet, one can do exactly as one pleases—This is exactly the place for me. Won't you please join me once your gallery is open? Or can you write me at the Ranch.

Your new venture should be a great success—Carroll [Carstairs] is an expert on modern pictures so do stick close to him until you can find your own feet.——It takes a long time to know the real from the fake!!! Or the good from the bad. We will talk this all over when we meet.

Essie is with Mary [Cass] Canfield in Maryland, putting the finishing touches on their play [*Ann of England*]. I have great hopes as I think they are both so talented.

All love, Jean darling, to you and Charlie. Please send me a line.

Linda

*In Arizona, 1938, left to right are
Constance Collier, a "Dude girl," Sturges,
a "Dude guy," Linda, and me.*

*Len (Leonard) Hanna was
the son of a Cleveland industrialist
and a friend of Cole's from Yale.*

*Roger Stearns was a pianist as
well as a friend and traveling
companion of the Porters.*

*It was Cleveland columnist
Winsor French who suggested Linda
look for a house in the
Williamstown area.*

THE WALDORF-ASTORIA
NEW YORK

Jan. 19/40

Jean darling:

We are off on our cruise tomorrow morning at the crack of dawn—& you don't know how glad I am to go and *how* I look forward to being *lazy*—I shall probably return looking much like Elsa Maxwell in size. Len Hanna, Bill Powell, Roger Stearns, Winsor French, S [Sturges], and I: Doesn't that sound nice? We will be gone seven weeks, returning to the Waldorf Mch. 15th—so please delay your trip East until then.

Essie, Mary & Tookie are in Charleston, S.C. where they have taken a house. You can reach Essie at Helen Astor's as all her mail is forwarded. Dearest love to you, Jean, & to Charlie. I wish you were going with us.

THE WALDORF-ASTORIA
NEW YORK

Oct. 25/38

Dearest Jean:

I was so happy to hear from you after such a long silence. Aren't you and Charlie coming East? You should, to see the wonderful new plays. Broadway is booming this year. So different from last. Sam and Frances Goldwyn have been here and I hear Sam has bought *Abraham Lincoln*. He did a good job. It is a magnificent play.

Coley is in Boston with his new show *Leave It to Me* which opens Nov. 2nd in N.Y. He comes home, I hope, on Thursday. The show has had excellent notices. I saw it in New Haven before any cuts were made and it was very amusing (but too long) and the score lovely. Victor Moore as the American ambassador in Russia is irresistible. The Spewacks wrote the book. You know how well they write. Pray for our success!! Heaven knows what our future plans are—I don't—or whether we will come to California. Coley is not signed up.

Sturges—your wonderful Sturges—is in Paris. Sailing soon, I think, for the U.S.A. We must all meet at the Ranch this winter in Arizona.

Essie and Mary have rented a house on Long Island and are very busy putting the finishing touches on their play which to my mind is *excellent*. They are very busy, so you must forgive Essie if she seems negligent. I hardly see her!

My love to you and Charlie, though I don't think he deserves our love as he never makes *any* effort to see me when he is in N.Y. Tell him this.

Linda

Bill Haines has great taste—I am sure your rooms are lovely. Write me what he has done.

Ethel Harriman — the Porters called her Ess or Essie.

Michael Pearman and I met the Porters, and each other, about the same time. He appeared in the chorus of Cole's 1935 show, Jubilee, under the name "Buddy Birmingham," so his very proper English parents would not know what he was doing. I still tease him, saying, "We were chorus girls together."

THE WALDORF-ASTORIA
NEW YORK

Saturday [September 1940]

Jeannie!

I think Charlie is perfectly charming—AND I think you should think so, too, as you are responsible for making him so! I still have not signed the papers for my house. There are endless complications as the Trustees (2 Bishops & 1 Clergyman) are living in the far corners of America, but I hope by Oct. 15th I will wrest this property away from the Church.

How are you? Give my love to Michael [Pearman]. Lots to you.

Linda

THE WALDORF-ASTORIA
NEW YORK

Saturday [October 1940]

Jeannie darling:

I sent you the [place]mats which you asked me to order. Please be a good girl & send your check *at once* to Eleanor Morton—they are poor people & *must* be paid *quickly!!* I hope you like the mats—I think them so attractive. I just got back from Cole's Boston opening——*Panama Hattie* is a HIT. Do come out for the opening & bring that nice Charlie.

I have not seen the Warners [Ann and Jack]. I will phone her next week—I suppose she is at the Waldorf. I like her *so* much. He is a problem —to me!

Mainbocher opens the end of Oct. I saw his new shop yesterday—it's divine! I also saw a few models. It seemed as though I was back in Paris. *Do* make an arrangement to be dressed by him—we will talk it over when you come East.

Elsie Mendl is charming. She is exactly like a mechanical doll. Charles Mendl is always asleep.

I *think* I sign the papers on Monday for the house. It has been held up because the title was not clear. But I have it, really, & will go to Williamstown directly when everything is settled.

"Funds for France" is impossible now—I talked to Sturges this morning —people simply will *not* contribute to my French charity—I think they are *right!* Unoccupied France is occupied by the Germans. And how can we help them? I, for one, don't want to.

All love darling Jean.

Linda

BUXTON HILL
WILLIAMSTOWN
MASSACHUSETTS

Thursday 12th [September 1940]

Jean darling:

This house is MINE—isn't that wonderful? I got it for nothing, & pray God! I won't spend a fortune doing it over. I want *so many things:* a guest house, a swimming pool, a new garage (the Barn) & lots of gardens. If I go bankrupt, you might buy it!!

I go Monday to N.Y.—so sad to leave this divine place, but work must begin *at once* so that my furniture can be moved from Beverly Hills— otherwise, storage. It is all there.

Cole is splendidly well. *Very* busy. Sturges phoned me last night. I will see him on my return.

Love, Jean darling, to you & Charlie. It was such a joy to have you for a visit. Please come next summer. All love,

Linda

Among the alterations Linda made in the "big house" at Buxton Hill (left) was the hanging of antique Chinese wallpaper from Knole Castle in England.

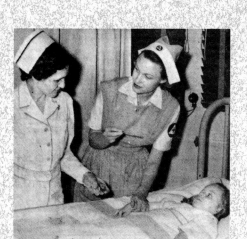

THE TOWERS
THE WALDORF-ASTORIA

Dec. 17 [1940]

Darling Jean:

You are *terrible*. You answer *no* letter. Then suddenly, one day, you wake up and write to ask *what* has happened! What has happened is that you *never* answer a letter.

Cole and Sturges are in Lima, Peru, having a wonderful time. They fly back to Peru, Indiana the 23rd when we all spend Xmas together.

I'm working hard on the house which won't be ready until the late spring. I have English paper for the big room—it's lovely—& the hall is entirely changed. You won't know it. There was very little else to do, but our alterations seem to take so long. My furniture will arrive in March from Hollywood —& then the racket begins. I wonder if it will kill me?—One never knows. You must come next summer and look it over.

My love, Jeannie darling, to you & Charlie.

Linda

I have seen Sylvia [Fairbanks], who seems always so sad, poor darling! [Douglas Fairbanks, Sr., had died in December 1939.]

THE TOWERS
THE WALDORF-ASTORIA

Sunday [postmarked 12/21/41]

Dearest Jean:

This is to wish you & Charlie *everything* good for the New Year! Bless you both.

Your Red Cross work sounds so interesting— *except* for getting up at 5 or 6 o'clock!! How do you do it?

Cole is splendid——he is out every night— theatres music etc.—in spite of a cast which must weigh *a ton*. I wish I had his energy.

All love, darling. It is hard to say Merry Xmas.

Linda

My Red Cross work was as a nurse's aid. The picture of me (above left), with a head nurse and patient, appeared on the front page of the Los Angeles Times in 1942.

W'stown

Aug. 15.43.

Dear Jeannie—
    This is everything that's wonderful. Linda is in top form & the place is all in Technicolor—
    I miss you lots & love you more.
    My best to Charlie et pour La Ess a beega goośe [sic].

             Your Slave—

             Cole.

BUXTON HILL
WILLIAMSTOWN
MASSACHUSETTS

             August 18 [1943]

Jeannie darling:
    Is Ess still with you? I am wondering when she will get back to Borden and the children at Vineyard Haven & how her 3rd Act is progressing. It must be great fun having her with you. She does, as you say, make a house come alive. Cole has that same wonderful quality! Give her my love.
    I wanted Main to come up for a weekend when he got back from California but he was too busy with his new collection, he has phoned several times—no mention of that Fox offer. Perhaps he didn't want to discuss it over the phone. Anyway, there is good basis for work in Hollywood, a difference of two weeks in a schedule should be [a] possible... arrangement & I know he wants awfully to give it a trial. Let's hope it works out. I won't mention this to anyone.
    Cole & Sturges came up for a long weekend after they *finally* got back from Mexico where they spent a very exciting two weeks. Coley looked well, but tired. No wonder! They missed plane connections in Brownsville, Texas & lost days on the return trip! I have turned Buxton Hill over to Coley and he invites whom he pleases for weekends. Last week we were entirely alone as he wanted to work but this Friday he is bringing Sturges & Ollie Jennings—and perhaps Kelly if he can leave his job for that length of time. I wish you were here, Jeannie, to see the changes I have made in the garden & grounds—the place is beginning to look RIGHT. Should you come to N.Y. before I close the house you must come up & see for yourself. I never think about the house—only about the shrubs & flowers and I do without clothes to buy them. Coley has been an angel & helped me out just as I was geting into debt. That was heaven.
    How is your picture career? When will *Claudia* be released? I am longing to see it, so let me know. Much love to you & Charlie.

           Linda

P.S. I hear Winsor arrives this week to visit his family—he still hasn't a job, poor soul!

In the picture above, I am signing autographs for soldiers visiting the set of the 1943 Fox film Claudia.

In the letter at left, Linda refers to Ollie (Oliver) Jennings, who was an old friend of Cole's from Yale. (Ray C.) Kelly worked for and traveled with Cole and was an intimate friend. In his will, Cole left the proceeds from half his music copyrights to Kelly and his children.

Below is a shot of the pool at Buxton Hill on a sunny afternoon.

THE WALDORF-ASTORIA
NEW YORK

September 8, 1944

Dear Bob-Cat:

Your beautiful photograph arrived. Certainly it's by far the best you have ever had taken. I have substituted it for the one that you gave me and you have no idea how much people admire it.

I'm way over my head on the Billy Rose show, but liking the job a great deal. I shan't ask you when you are coming to New York as I know perfectly well that none of your plans ever materialize.

Sturge and I go every Friday to Williamstown and return every Tuesday. Now and then he is untrue to us and can't resist Newport and Narragansett. He still works in the bowels of the Pennsylvania Station [at the Red Cross Canteen] and how he survives I don't know, as he gives large fashionable luncheons every day at the Colony.

Linda is in wonderful form in spite of almost constant butler trouble. The last one who left said "I'm giving you notice, Madam. I'm tired of the mountains and want to work on the seashore from now on for several months."

Bea Lillie arrives September 10th and we go into rehearsal [for *Seven Lively Arts*] October 2nd.

I can't tell you how much I miss your beautiful face. Give my love to that big Swede [Greta Garbo] and ask her whether she ever received a book from me, or not. You might add that it's the custom in this country to acknowledge gifts.

A big kiss from

Cole

WESTERN UNION

MRS. CHARLES FELDMAN

OCTOBER 9, 1944

DEAR LITTLE JEANNIE. WHERE IN NEW YORK CAN I TRACK DOWN THAT BEAUTIFUL SWEDE [GARBO]. BE A GOOD GIRL. LOVE—COLE

THE BARCLAY
Rittenhouse Square East
Philadelphia

November 29, 1944

Dear Jeannie:

Thank you so much for the wire regarding the broadcast and the opening.

The show is wonderful and I have never had such a nice experience in the theatre as with the curious little Billy Rose. He tops any producer that I have ever worked with.

I am so sorry you won't be here for that little opening in New York.

In the meantime don't forget that I love you dearly and miss you between every minute.

Your old sweetheart

Cole

At Buxton Hill the Porters took long afternoon drives through the country, often visiting Grandma Moses to buy pictures when she was just becoming known.

"Don't Fence Me In" was based on a poem by Robert Fletcher. Cole had originally written it for the unproduced film Adios Argentina in 1934. Ten years later it was introduced by Roy Rogers and the Sons of the Pioneers and reprised on screen by the Andrews Sisters in Hollywood Canteen.

Michael Pearman

THE WALDORF-ASTORIA
NEW YORK

December 12, 1944

Dear Jean:

Your beautiful answer to the Moses picture arrived.

You ask me how I ever guessed you wanted one and my answer is: that for five months you hinted for one every time I saw you, as you coyly lowered your eyes and twisted your pretty foot in my little Brentwood garden. I didn't have time to reframe it, but I'm sure that you will have some brilliant idea.

The opening was SOMETHING. It's not fashionable to like "DON'T FENCE ME IN," but I suppose that old Texas blood of yours comes forth and you accept it.

As usual, the Press tried to run me out of town but I know that the last one is the best job I have done for years, so I am not depressed.

We see Michael constantly and he is a joy.

Lots of love to you, dear Jeannie,

Cole.

Cole and Bob Bray

Mr. and Mrs. Ray C. Kelly

The three pictures at bottom right are from a dinner party Cole gave at his house in Brentwood for Ray Kelly and his wife, about 1946.

Sam Stark was a former actor who went into the jewelry business. He shared Linda's love of beautiful things and Cole's sense of humor.

I took this picture (at the top, far right) of Leslie Bradley and his wife, Dorothy, in Venice during the filming of Prince of Foxes, in which he was acting.

Samuel Stark and Howard Sturges

THE TOWERS
THE WALDORF-ASTORIA

Monday, 13th [1946]

Jeannie darling:
   I am off to Williamstown early Wednesday morning for the Spring planting, and hope to see all the apple trees in full bloom! I return on Sunday to spend the rest of the month in N.Y. with Cole. He leaves May 31st for Hollywood, and June 1st Weston and I motor to Buxton Hill for four solid months, where I hope to regain my strength. It comes back *so* slowly—the least thing tires me. And I do practically NOTHING.
   How are you? Did your two weeks at Tahoe do you infinite good? *Please* come any time in August for a visit, and stay as long as you can. *How* I should adore having you! Write me if and when you will appear.

Love to you and Charlie,

Linda

Leslie and Dorothy Bradley

FROM: COLE PORTER

Feb. 17, 1949

Mrs. Jean Howard,
c/o Duc di Verdura,
156 E. 56th Street,
New York, New York.

Dearest Jeannie:
   Upon receipt of your wire I immediately telephoned to New York, to the producers' office, and got you two seats for next Friday, February 18th. I have wired you to that effect. Some day, before you die, let me know whether you ever received the seats.

Love,

Cole

CP:me

P.S. There is no hurry!

FROM: COLE PORTER
THE WALDORF-ASTORIA
NEW YORK

December 17, 1948

Dear Jeannie:
   Michael tells me that you have become a friend of Leslie Bradley and his wife. Probably Leslie doesn't want his beginnings known, but for several years he was my valet, and an excellent one. Then he went to the Riviera on a vacation and came back from it suddenly looking like Adonis, and left me to go into pictures in England. It makes me very happy to know that he has done so well, as he is one of the nicest people I ever knew. Give him my best, and lots of love to you and Slim [Aarons].

Cole

P.S.—My new show [*Kiss Me Kate*] opened in Philadelphia and is the biggest hit of my life. But all the fun has been spoiled as, immediately after the opening, Linda contracted pneumonia and is living at the Doctors Hospital in an oxygen tent. She is better, however, and will definitely recover.

Me, Paul Flato, and Fulco di Verdura

21

Linda had gone, with her nurse, by train to Arizona in December of 1948 and stayed there until the end of April. Cole visited her several times and arranged for others to visit as well, including Len Hanna, Winsor French, Constance Collier, and Celia Vom Rath.

Elsa Maxwell (below) in Rome with her favorite statue by Verrocchio.

LINDA PORTER

March 31st [1949]

Darling Jean:

I move tomorrow to El Conquistador Hotel in Tucson to spend the month of April, by which time I hope to be entirely well. What a *bore* illness is! Just time wasted.

Cole said you *might* come to Tucson. I wish you would, if you can stand the dullness. I *long* to see you & to hear all about your trip.

Fondest love, Jean darling,

Linda

THE TOWERS
THE WALDORF-ASTORIA

Friday 19th [1950]

Jeannie darling:

It was a sad blow to me when you lost that baby. *Nothing* would be better for you than to have a child & my great hope is that you will try again as soon as you are stronger. How do you feel? Is there a chance of coming to N.Y.

I am just recovering from a six week's bout with pneumonia & a horrid experience it was—& is, since I am *so* slow in regaining my strength. I still see practically no one, & go out seldom for a drive of 1½ hrs each afternoon. Then home to bed! Everything has piled up—there is *so* much to be done before I go to the country that I am *appalled!!* Can I face it, is the question.

Cole leaves Sunday for Boston where the new show [*Out of This World*] opens Friday of that week. Pray for a success.

Dearest love to you & Charlie,

BUXTON HILL
WILLIAMSTOWN
MASSACHUSETTS

Sept. 4 [1949]

Jean dear:

Two nice postcards—I was delighted to hear from you! You must have loved the Riviera with all your friends about—and Elsa—but I am sure Rome will fascinate you; it is such an enchanting spot and, according to Sturges, much more attractive at this present moment than Paris. In fact, *everyone* says so. Life is easier, living is cheaper, people are gayer. By now, you have found out for yourself.

This has been a curious summer, over almost before it began! It is cool now, autumn in the air, but a short week ago blistering heat.

Cole arrives back at the Waldorf on the 7th—I shall go down to meet him and spend several days before returning to Buxton Hill. I must also get a house maid as mine walked off on the 1st. Dear me! Running a house is a problem. I am *fed up with* it.

All love, dear Jeannie. Have a good time!!!

Linda

Sunday night, Sept. 5th, 49

Jean—

I wrote to Bob Bray tonight & told him that you had asked *me* to tell *him* to phone *you*, any day, during the week, at noon. So please don't leave instructions with your *Personal Maid* to say, when he calls, "She says she's out!"

If you can find time, I beg you, see him, if only for a moment. He is so alone & lonely. And it is most important for him to be with a lady instead of a Tramp. Do this for me.

The Linda news is far from good. Today, it was very humid here & to watch her struggle to breathe was terrifying.

Sturges comes back next Tuesday to be here in my cottage. This will build her up more than any amount of oxygen.

I miss you, dear Jeannie. I always miss you & love you.

Your

Cole

September 13, 1949

Dear Jeannie:

Your wonderful letter arrived and amused me so much that I gave it first to Essie to read and later to Linda. When I saw them at lunch time instead of being as enthusiastic as I was, they were furious and said with one voice, "but she never writes *us* letters like that!"

Robert writes me that he is having lunch with you tomorrow and I am so glad. I can't tell you how much he wanted to be with nice people.

Ess came up, stayed the night, and for lunch the next day, and then went back to see poor Boy [Ethel's son, Charles Russell] who, as you probably know, had an awful automobile accident.

Between you and me, Linda is not getting at all better.

I miss you a lot, dear Jeannie. Let me know when you return to town. I stay here with Linda until the end of October.

Your devoted,

Cole

Sept. 11th

Jeannie darling:

Ess sent a postcard from Martha's Vineyard saying she had arrived back & was writing—since then, no word.—I suppose she is very busy finishing her play for autumn production: has she a producer? Or one in mind? I do hope she succeeds. Goodness knows she has worked hard enough. If that means anything in the theatrical world! I am longing to see her—but when? I don't go back to N.Y. until the end of October. Buxton Hill is so lovely I never want to leave it & dread the approaching winter.

Main's collection was shown on Thursday— several people, including Nin [Ryan], called me up saying it was the best he [Mainbocher] had *ever* made. Perfectly beautiful wearable clothes. (Excuse blots. Something went wrong with the blotter.) I talked with him on the phone and he seemed delighted. Has anything happened about the Fox

---

(Sept. 11th, cont.)

offer? It sounded perfectly possible to me if they have met most of his terms: Surely he can get away for a few weeks longer, if necessary, with Douglas to handle the N.Y. business. He will probably talk to me about it when I see him.

Don't tell me Elsa [Maxwell] is *still* talking about her book! She has been writing it ever since I first met her a good 100 years ago. She read it chapter by chapter to *everyone*—we know it by heart. What is she doing? Isn't Mrs. [Ned] McLean a wonderful freak? I adore her. Love, Jeannie darling, to you & Charlie.

Linda

P.S. Are you coming East—when? You *must* come up here. The autumn is so beautiful and we should adore having you for as long as you can stay.

April 9, 1953

Dearest Jean:

Thank you for your letter dated "Sunday"—which Sunday?

Please plan to stay longer in California. At present, it looks as if I would hit the Coast around the 10th of May, as I believe *Can-Can* will be put off another week before opening in New York. We are going through constant rewriting in Philadelphia, and cutting. On the opening night in Philadelphia, the show was 45 minutes too long, and it is very tough to take 45 minutes out of a show and still have a show left. In any case, we are all working very well together and I am devoted to Abe Burrows and the two producers.

I took Linda out for a drive last Sunday, as it was such a glorious day here. I took her up to Harlem to see the Easter hats on parade, and suddenly she began to suffocate. I got her back here as soon as possible, and she went into her oxygen tent. By evening her temperature was three degrees over normal, and the nurses had to be called again, to be there around the clock. This is most discouraging for her as it looked as if she had entirely recovered two weeks ago, after having been seriously ill since February 1st. I wonder constantly at her great courage.

I have no idea why Sturges hung up so suddenly the other night when I called you from Williamstown. Perhaps it was because I hadn't warned him that I was calling you and he was already too sleepy to make sense. He flew off to Switzerland last Sunday, to be met by Christos [Bellos], who drove him immediately to Cannes. This proves once again what Linda and I have always maintained, which is that he hates Paris and always devises some means of being elsewhere.

I pine to see you and I do hope that when I arrive you will give me a little of your precious time.

My love to you both.

Your fan,

Cole

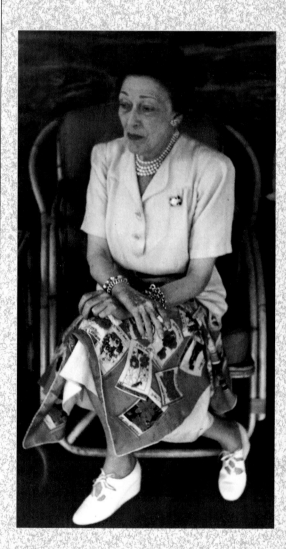

*The picture at right was the last taken of Linda.
I took it on one of my last visits with her at Buxton Hill;
her illness is visible upon her. The scarf on her lap
was for her little dog, Gracie.*

*Linda died on May 20. Cole had flown back from California,
where he had been for the filming of* Kiss Me Kate, *to be with her.
I remember standing on the steps
of the church, across from the Waldorf Towers, watching
the gray hearse as it carried her up Park Avenue toward
the airport for the trip to Peru, Indiana. She would
be buried one grave away from Cole's mother,
Kate. Cole reserved the space
between for himself.*

FROM: COLE PORTER

THE TOWERS OF
THE WALDORF-ASTORIA
NEW YORK

Dec. 31, 1953

Dearest Jeannie:

This is to wish you a HAPPY NEW YEAR. Sturges has probably written you
that we have planned to arrive in St. Moritz March 2nd, and you will probably
be in Cold Water Canyon. But if you could possibly wait over a bit and
become our guide, we would be most grateful.

Linda's health varies so much from day to day that it is difficult to report
about her. Her night nurse, however, who was absent for two weeks, has
returned, and tells me that she finds that in that time Linda has lost ground.
The most disturbing fact is that her heart has begun to act up. She has had
two slight attacks, during which her pulse was much too high. To rectify this,
her Doctor is giving her Digitalis. The sum-total of her maladies is so great
that I wonder she has any courage left at all, and just before Christmas she
broke a rib from coughing too hard.

My life here is as usual—I work hard in the daytime and go to a show or an
opera or a party at night. Strangely enough, the new production of
Tannhauser at the Met. is the best presentation of it I have seen since I was a
child, in Munich.

We think about you both and talk about you constantly; and, by the way,
Linda and Sturges and I have decided that you write the best letters in the
world. Where did you get this beautiful literary style?

Lots of love,

Cole

*Linda always gave Cole
a cigarette case to celebrate the opening of
each of his shows on Broadway. As the premier
of* Silk Stockings *neared, Sturges suggested that
several of his friends present Cole with an
opening-night case in Linda's memory.*

*Fulco di Verdura designed it (above, right)
in gold with two Russian coins. Engraved inside
were the words "In Memory of Linda," with
each of our signatures: Niki (Baron
Nicholas de Gunzberg, Fulco,
Natasha (Princess Paley),
Sturges, and Jean.*

WESTERN UNION

MR AND MRS CHAS FELDMAN—

MAY 17, 1954

DEAR JEANNIE AND CHARLIE THANK HEAVEN I GOT
HERE IN TIME BUT LINDA IS VERY CRITICALLY ILL
LOVE = COLE =

FROM: COLE PORTER

June 8, 1954

Dear Jean:
Thank you so much for the lovely flowers you
sent for Linda's burial.

Love,

Cole

Sir Charles Mendl (then the British press attaché to Paris), William Crocker (Cole's friend from Yale and namesake of the lead character in Anything Goes*), Cole, and Linda at Angel Bay on the French Riviera in 1921.*

aFTER LINDA'S DEATH in the spring of 1954, I would visit Cole in Williamstown for long weekends during the winter. He continued to live in his own little cottage, and he could not bear to see the big house sitting empty, calling up memories and making him more than ever aware of his loss. He eventually had it demolished at the cost of $100,000, a huge sum at the time. Forever after, it was a shock to me to look toward the house and find it gone. Nor did its removal lessen Cole's grief.

By the fall of 1954, Cole was still despondent over Linda's death. It was heartbreaking to see him in this dark state. One day, when I was lunching with Cole and Howard Sturges at the Colony, the two men began to talk of Linda and a journey the three had once made to Egypt. As they talked, their voices became almost happy, and their eyes seemed to glow with remembering.

Thinking to cheer them up, suddenly I heard myself saying, "Why don't we three take a trip?" The both looked at me for a long moment. Cole spoke first, "Great!" Sturges said, "When do we start?" When I made the suggestion that we take a trip (and God knows it came from the blue), I had no idea that it would ever happen. Cole said that we should "aim" for sometime in February. It was then November!

Somewhere along in December, Cole called to make a lunch date to talk about the trip and to say that he had worked out an itinerary and wanted to see if it was agreeable to me. We were to leave on February 19 from Zurich, Switzerland, and finish the trip in Athens on June 1, after a two-week cruise of the Greek islands. He said that he hadn't yet found a suitable boat for the island, but "never mind," he was working on it. It seemed too exciting for words.

A few nights later, I was dining with my ex-husband, Charles Feldman, and David Selznick at El Morocco when Stavros Niarchos came over to our table and joined us. Charlie and I had met Mr. Niarchos the summer before. At some point during the conversation, I told Mr. Niarchos that I was very excited at the thought of seeing his country and the Greek islands. He asked when and how I was going to do this. I told him that Cole was arranging to get a boat, whereupon he amazed not only me but Charlie and David as well by saying that there was only one possible way to cruise the Greek islands, and that was on one of his yachts. He was most insistent. After Mr. Niarchos left the table, the three of us looked at each other and asked, "Did he really mean it, or had he had too much wine?"

When I returned to my apartment that night, I broke a Porter rule (never ring after 1:00 A.M.) and telephoned him at 2:45 A.M. to tell him what had happened. He was skeptical;

however, he would invite the Niarchoses for lunch that week, which he did. He also invited Howard Sturges and me. Naturally, the planned trip popped into the conversation, and Mr. Niarchos repeated to Cole what he had said to me a few nights earlier. And that is how we happened to "do" the Greek islands in the greatest luxury and comfort.

Linda once said to me, "Don't try to understand Cole." Howard Sturges said the same thing. They were so right. The saying goes that you never know a person until you've married him. I say you never know a person until you've *traveled* with him.

I adored Cole, and I had always found him a delight. He was very lively, and he had a charming way of bringing other people "out" at parties. Of course if they came *too* far "out," and stayed on too long, he also had a way of "turning off," which confused many people. Cole had a light touch, and he was great at turning a phrase, but he was never one for long conversations as such. His mind was very often on his music, which accounted for his long silences, the faraway look in his eyes, or blank stare.

To travel with him was another matter. Many itineraries were sent out—I have found at least four among my letters from Cole—and by the time the *final* one arrived, I was beginning to have second thoughts about the whole thing. I found it strange, and a bit frightening, as I looked through it and saw that at *exactly* 10:00 A.M. on March 31 we were to be ready to motor from Agrigento via Gela to Piazza Armerina! How did I know how I was going to feel on March 31? (In fact, the itinerary did change again—we ended up in Madrid on March 31—but the attention to detail and exactness of schedule was a constant throughout the trip.) As I read these strange names and places, a bit of doubt began to creep into my mind as to whether I should be taking this trip or not. But with Cole Porter, there just was no way to back out—especially at this point.

Friends of Sturges's and Cole's were to meet us at certain points in the journey. Bob Bray (perhaps best known as Lassie's last master), Cole's last intimate friend, joined our little group, but he could never stay long at a time. Periodically, he would fly back to Los Angeles to be with his family and to work, and then he would join us again. My ex-husband, Charlie, who often traveled to Europe on film business, arranged to meet me in Monte Carlo and Madrid. I flew to Zurich on February 17, accompanied by Marti Stevens, who would pop up occasionally at various points on the trip. Cole and Sturges flew over a few days later, and so began the most exciting, frustrating, exhausting, and memorable three months of my life.

Billy Reardon, Linda, and Cole at St. Moritz in the 1920s.

THE FIRST TRIP 1955

Cole and Linda visiting Paris in the 1930s.

switzerland

FEBRUARY 17: I arrived in Zurich with Marti Stevens, who flew over with me from New York.

FEBRUARY 21: Cole and Sturges landed in Zurich in a blinding snowstorm, two-and-a-half hours late. I thought they would be too tired to dine out tonight. Sturges was, but not Cole. We dined in the bar at the Hotel Baur au Lac, where we are staying. Cole almost too gay! I think he is keyed up nervously from hard work on his new show Silk Stockings, *which is scheduled to open in New York on the 24th. For some reason the critics are always unkind to Cole, and he made up his mind years before to get out of town before his opening nights on Broadway. Perhaps he has become superstitious—as most show folks do. Later we went to his apartment for drinks, where we stayed until 2:30 A.M.*

FEBRUARY 22: I went shopping with Cole. He bought an ice bucket and a very large cup for his morning coffee. Paul Sylvain, Cole's valet, had forgotten to pack Cole's regular cup in his thirty-some pieces of luggage!—JH

Much of the luggage contained the medical supplies needed to change the dressings on Cole's injured legs, twice daily. The bags were numbered, and Paul had a notebook in which he kept track of the contents of each.

On February 23 we went to St. Moritz, where we stayed at the Palace Hotel, for years known as the most fashionable resort hotel in the world. In St. Moritz the nights were late. A highlight was breakfast on the sunny deck of the very exclusive Chesa Veglia, a converted seventeenth-century farmhouse located behind and above the hotel, which owns and operates it. Here a select few sat on hard benches at uncovered wooden tables, ate a piping hot breakfast served with steaming coffee, and gossiped about the events of the night before. The arrival of someone like Cole Porter added to the excitement. He was welcomed there with open arms. As Cole often said of himself, "I am not a snob, I only like the best."

The hectic schedule sometimes wore on the tempers in our group, but rarely on Cole's. I remember at one point Howard Sturges was in his room on the telephone to Rome, trying to confirm our reservations. He was shouting into the receiver when Cole stepped through the door and made some glib remark, whereupon Sturges stood up and, grabbing the phone with both hands, threw it straight at Cole, who got out of the room as fast as he could.

Far left: The view from my hotel room in Zurich.

Left, top to bottom: On the deck at Chesa Veglia: Cole with Noel (Mrs. Bebino) Salinas.

"Mo-Mo," Mrs. Warren Pershing, daughter-in-law of General George Pershing, with man-about-town John Galliher.

Two handsome Greeks, Christos Bellos and Andy Embericos.

Howard Sturges with Eugenie Niarchos.

Right: Enjoying the view from the deck are Lord Warwick, Andy Embericos, and Stavros Niarchos.

FEBRUARY 25: *Cole received this glowing telegram from his good friend and music editor, Dr. Albert Sirmay, telling him that* Silk Stockings *was a hit:* "OPENING GIGANTIC SUCCESS BROOKS ATKINSON RAVING ESPECIALLY ABOUT WORDS AND MUSIC ALL OTHER PAPERS SIMPLY WONDERFUL ABE BURROWS AND CY HAVE ACHIEVED A THEATRICAL MIRACLE AUDIENCE MOST ELEGANT IN YEARS GRETCHEN WYLER STOPPED SHOW TWICE WITH JOSEPHINE AND STEREOPHONIC YOU HAVE EVERY REASON TO BE HAPPY AND PROUD LOVE AND KISSES = SIRMAY." *Cole was elated.—JH*

Clockwise from left: At the skating rink in St. Moritz, I photographed Jean Cocteau with his companion, a very attractive woman by the name of Madame Alex Weisweiller. Cocteau was very excited about whether or not he would win a seat on the French Academy. Some time later, the sixty-five-year-old poet, playwright, painter, and novelist discovered that he had been elected a member of the Academy.

Around March 6, I went to Klosters to see some friends. Anatole Litvak was making a film there, *The Deep Blue Sea* with Vivien Leigh. I photographed them on a ski lift during a break from filming.

While in Klosters I also photographed another friend, one of America's best writers, Irwin Shaw, with his son, Adam.

From St. Moritz we motored to Milan on March 11. At the Italian border the customs man looked at all our luggage and asked, "Is this the *whole* band?"

We went to the opera *La Sonnambula* by Vincenzo Bellini, conducted by Leonard Bernstein, staged by Luchino Visconti, and sung by Maria Callas. I was impressed with La Scala—Teatro della Scala—small in comparison to the Met. I wrote in my notes: "Callas wonderful voice, not bad looking, taking queenly bows, actually a laughable opera. . . . Photographed Leonard Bernstein—Heaven knows what I got of him; the light was very poor." The light was indeed too poor: I got nothing.

We also went to the ballet *Till Eulenspiegel* by Richard Strauss with Jean Babilee, which was excellent. Margot Fonteyn danced "Firebird."

From Milan Cole wrote to his friend and biographer George Eells, describing in detail the manner in which we were traveling:

We're well organized for our trek to the west (Portugal). For touring there is a 1955 red-leather-lined Cadillac. (I suddenly realized day before yesterday that I had ordered it red-leather-lined because when Pep and Berthe [Cole's dogs] make spots from their privates, it's so easy to wash leather. But Pep isn't here, nor is Berthe.) There is also a Pontiac station wagon. In this goes the luggage—so far 37 pieces—with Luigi and Paul on the front seat. On top of the Cadillac there is a super-rack for extra luggage and it is held on by suction. This means that when one arrives somewhere and doesn't want to have a super-rack, one presses a button, there's no suction anymore, and everything is respectable again—no more rack—I don't understand this.

To continue, in the trunk of the Cadillac is my collapsible wheelchair. This means that, with the aid of Luigi, Paul, and Bob, I can be carried up and down all the staircases and then wheeled around and around. The result is, as we have been sightseeing every day, that Luigi, Paul, and Robert all come back to the hotel exhausted wrecks, and I'm still fresh and raring to go.

This Luigi is a great chauffeur from Rome and highly recommended, but when I first saw him I was shocked by his clothes and also because he looked so much like Jackie Gleason. Sturge and I took him to a chauffeur's shop to get him the proper uniform to the last detail. He still looks like Jackie Gleason.

Today, we drove to Bergamo, the magic city on the hill, and tomorrow we lunch in Turin where I shall be carried upstairs again to see beautiful treasures. I believe you would like seeing all these treasures. They're all so far from Fleur Cowles [Eells's editor at *Look* magazine].

Best, Cole.

ITALY

MARCH 13: *Marti flew in from St. Moritz, feeling better but still weak from the flu.*

MARCH 14: *Bob Bray arrived from California today. Cole and Sturges return [from Paris, where they went for a few days when the rest of us got sick] tomorrow in time to depart for Monte Carlo.*

MARCH 15: *Bob Bray sick with flu. I was in bed all day—bad sore throat. We were supposed to leave today. Happy C. [Charles Feldman] is in Paris.*

MARCH 17: *We left Milan by car. Stopped at Pavia to look at a lovely church and monastery, Cetosa di Povia, founded by Galezzo Visconti in 1396. Ile Certosa.*

We arrived in Genova where Sturges and I walked a couple of hours. There they had one-way sidewalks, which impressed me very much. I liked the Hotel Colombia, and Genova.—JH

Left: Marti in front of Teatro della Scala. With its legendary acoustics, it seemed the perfect place to photograph a singer.

Right: Marti took this picture of me in the Piazza del Duomo, with Milan Cathedral in the background. Begun in 1386, it was finally completed five centuries later. Upon viewing its 135 spires and more than 2,000 marble statues, Swiss historian Jacob Burckhardt called it "a transparent marble mountain."

SOUTH OF FRANCE

MARCH 18: *We left Genova after 12 o'clock lunch and arrived at Monte Carlo. There Charlie Feldman (looking so well) met us and took us to dinner.*

MARCH 19: *Damn! The flu again. Apparently never got rid of it in Milan. Stayed in bed twenty-four hours.*

MARCH 20: *Went with Charlie to see Italian producer Dino di Laurentiis. Also met René Clément. Photographed Charlie, Di Laurentiis, and Clément in the Di Laurentiis garden—a beautiful spot. Marti arrived from Milan today.*

MARCH 21: *Haven't seen Cole since the first night we arrived. Sturges came to my room for a short visit today. I tried to see Somerset Maugham but was told he was ill and couldn't be photographed. Charlie went back to Paris today.*

MARCH 22: *Went to Vence for lunch. Later we went to Matisse chapel. Photographs were not allowed, but I took a couple without being seen. I was most impressed.*

MARCH 23: *We stopped at Dickie [Fellowes-] Gordon's charming house in Arubue—delicious lunch! Arrived in Aix-en-Provence at 5 P.M. We stopped for tea on the way. Aix is a charming town. The main street has great sycamore trees—lovely! Talked to Charlie in Paris and Marti in Monte Carlo, where she is still ill!*

MARCH 24: *Very interesting driving through Provence country—cypress trees and cut grapevines, black in the earth. Reminded of many Van Gogh paintings. This was the country that he painted a great deal—all around Arles. We lunched with Cole's friend Bebino (Bepi) Salinas, near Les Beau. We spent the night in Montpellier.* —JH

Left: Dino di Laurentiis, Charlie, and René Clément.

Right, top to bottom: Cole, Sturges, Bob, an unknown gentleman, and Dickie Fellowes-Gordon.

The three of us in Aix. The brown jersey stocking cap I am wearing was given to me by Greta Garbo, who had taken me to Valentina's that January to help me choose something warm for the trip. I still remember her voice calling me from across the street, and heads turning to look as she crossed. She was very gay, and we had lots of fun trying on all kinds of funny little hats. Later we went for drinks with George Schlee, Valentina's husband.

Bepi Salinas, Cole, me, Bepi's son, Sturges, and Noel Salinas.

Far right: The interior of the Chapel of the Rosary in Vence, designed by Henri Matisse. The chapel was consecrated in 1951 and is part of a Dominican convent.

MARCH 25: *Spain. First night in S'Agaró, a lovely place on the Costa Brava, at the Hostal de la Gavina, a heavenly spot. Lovely walk along the sea—white beaches, small, with dark green pine trees. Dali has a place about an hour away. We were not stopped very long at the border. On the Spanish side, one of the soldiers came out with Cole's passport in his hand, looked in the car, and said, 'Cole Porter! . . . Begin the Beguine!' and kissed his fingers to the air, and began to sing the song. Cole's music is known everywhere we go—even in remote spots.*
MARCH 26: *Tonight the village folk came up and entertained us with melodies and dances called the* sardanas—*it is said that they date from the time the Greeks were in Spain. All this was arranged for Cole. He was most gracious.*
MARCH 27: *Left S'Agaró after lunch and arrived in Barcelona about 3 o'clock. Bob Bray and I went to the bullfights. They were thrilling. We stayed at the Ritz Hotel—I had a hard bed and never slept better.*
MARCH 28: *We left Barcelona and arrived in Zaragoza.*
MARCH 29: *Arrived in Madrid. We couldn't get reservations at the Ritz and so have an ugly new hotel called the Fenix— awful—some tempers flared today—traveling nerves.*
MARCH 30: *Edgar Neville [a Spanish friend of Charles Feldman's, and also of Charlie Chaplin's] took us to the restaurant Valentine and later to see some* flamenco *dancers. This is the first evening I've enjoyed for some time.*
MARCH 31: *Charlie arrived today—four hours late. Neville gave a dinner for Cole, but Cole was ill and couldn't (simply wouldn't) go. Poor Neville—the dinner was an awful bust.*
—JH

The fact was that Cole had had enough of Edgar Neville, who was trying *too* hard to please.

It was somewhere along here (between Barcelona and Madrid, I believe) that Cole looked back from the front seat and hummed the melody of "True Love." I told him that I thought that song would be one of his biggest hits. He said, "You're crazy." When the song came out, it was nominated for the Academy Award, which it didn't win, but it *was* one of Cole's biggest hits.

Unfortunately our last week in Madrid passed in something of a blur, with most of these days spent in illness and tension with Charlie, who wanted me to leave the trip and go home with him. I simply couldn't disappoint Cole— although I really wanted, at this point, to cut out.

Clockwise, from left: Along the Costa Brava (the name means "Wild Coast").

Sometime-writer Edgar Neville, with the beautiful Dolores Del Rio, at his home in Madrid.

The bullfights at Barcelona.

Spain & Portugal

APRIL 9: *We arrived in Lisbon. Hotel Avis—small, charming. Charlie still not feeling too well and complaining, especially about the size of my room. He has gone around the whole of this small hotel checking rooms—they are all small! Cole dined with us. Tension in the air. Charlie and I spent afternoon at beach called Estoril, where he pleaded for me to leave the trip.*

APRIL 10: *Sturges went to Paris today for a couple of weeks. He is supposed to meet us in Rome on the 28th. We all lunched today with the Gulbenkians. They are said to be the richest people in the world. The family here is waiting for the father to die. They have the entire top floor of the Avis Hotel. Dined with Cole, José Ferrer, and Charlie.*

APRIL 11: *Charlie left for Paris today, late. We lunched at Estoril. Beautiful weather. Dined alone and to bed early.*

APRIL 12: *Lunched with Cole and Bob Bray. Later went sightseeing. Loved the old coaches. Drinks with Lord and Lady Radcliff. Dinner near Estoril. Enjoyed Cole today more than any time since we started out.*—JH

Clockwise from top left: Nubar Gulbenkian in his diplomatic uniform as cultural attaché to the Iranian Embassy in London. His father, Calouste Sarkis Gulbenkian, the Armenian oil tycoon, was known as "Mr. 5 Percent." Calouste Gulbenkian became the richest man in the world by paving the way for the big oil consortiums in the Middle East. He lived in Lisbon from 1942 until his death about six months after our visit.

Lisbon has the largest collection of coaches in the world, dating from the late fifteenth century through Victorian times. Pictured here is a detail of an eighteenth-century gilded coach.

Henry May and his sister.

The restaurant on the beach at Estoril, a suburb about fifteen miles west of Lisbon. Estoril became famous as the home of many European royals exiled during World II.

Belém (Portuguese for Bethlehem) is another suburb of Lisbon. These pictures were taken at Torre de Belém *(above left)*, a uniquely Portuguese variation on the late Gothic style in architecture. Built in the early 1500s as a fortress, it was used as a prison from 1580 to 1828. The building originally sat out in the Tagus River, completely surrounded by water, but as the river changed its course the entire building was "washed up on shore." Restored in 1846, it now houses a permanent exhibition of fifteenth- and sixteenth-century weapons and navigational instruments.

Below left: Bob Bray (left) and Cole with our guide. Luigi holds my hat while I take pictures.

Right: Early in the trip I made a distressing discovery. In my diary I wrote: "Cole doesn't like to be photographed, and this is frustrating for me as there are so many places that I want to photograph where he happens to be—but I loathe photographing someone who doesn't want it." This day was an exception. Not only did Cole seem not to mind, he even made funny faces for the camera.

COCKLESHELL HEROES
PROD^S

SC. 104 TA..

DIRECTOR CAMERAMAN
J. FERRER T. MOORE

EXT. SILENT

APRIL 13: *Most exhausting day I've spent. Drove miles. We left the hotel at 12:30 P.M. and returned at 7:30. Drove miles again to get to dinner. If I see another lobster I'll start pinching people!* APRIL 14: A *visit to the José Ferrer set [of* Cockleshell Heroes]. *Fishing people living near. Photographed all.* —JH

As an agent and producer, Charlie Feldman had clients and associates living and working all over the world. He was in Europe on business during this time, which enabled him to meet up with us at various places. He had left Lisbon for Paris in order to see Anatole Litvak. Later he would visit Orson Welles in Spain, Tyrone Power and Vittorio de Sica in Rome, and John Huston in London. In Portugal he had had meetings with José Ferrer, which is how our group later came to visit the set of *Cockleshell Heroes*.

Left: José Ferrer directing the filming of *Cockleshell Heroes*. He also starred in the film, along with Trevor Howard (*below right*).

Above right: Bob Bray with José and his third wife, singer Rosemary Clooney, during lunch on the set.

Left: I am standing before one of the many windmills for which Portugal is famous.

   Right: Two Portuguese locals, at work and at play.

APRIL 15: *Fado party arranged for Cole [by a public-relations person]. Later, Cole had Eddie Fisher, Debbie Reynolds and her mother, Fisher's piano accompanist, and his agent for dinner. After dinner the ex-king of Italy, Umberto, came to greet Cole. He had beautiful manners and I thought him charming. The king never sat down, which meant that everybody else had to stand. Thank heaven he only stayed about twenty minutes. We had started out at 5 P.M. I returned to my room at 2 A.M.— exhausted again.—JH*

The word *fado* means "fate" in Portuguese. It also refers to a kind of folk art involving music and dance, developed over hundreds of years, which is to Portugal what *flamenco* is to Spain. It reminds me of our country music. Lovely, sad songs tell sorrowful stories to the accompaniment of several guitars—I love it.

APRIL 16: *Cole, Bob Bray, and Henry May went to Bussaco today. Spent day alone. Dined alone tonight.*
APRIL 17: *Finally landed back in Madrid today after long-delayed flight. The day spent wandering about—dined with Neville—would have been better if I'd stayed with the boys.*
APRIL 20: *Dinner with Cole. He is making an effort to be gay. He's good at it.*
—JH

I was alone in Madrid. I was waiting for Cole to return so I could tell him that I was thinking of going to Sevilla for a few days of the *feria*. A old friend from New York, John Goodwin, had invited me but I couldn't make up my mind whether to go or not.

When Cole and Bob got back to Madrid, I told Cole that I was going to Sevilla, not knowing that Bob was returning to California to take a part in the movie *Bus Stop*. When I did tell Cole my plans, he decided to fly to Paris because Sturges was there. Cole felt that I had let him down, and I was in a state of confusion.

On April 21 Cole left for Paris and I went to Sevilla, where I stayed until the 24th. The *feria* (fair) is a week of nonstop revelry following the seven nights of Semana Santa (Passion Week). The senoritas wear traditional polka-dot dresses and dance the *sevillana* in the plaza. The sounds of castanets, guitars, *flamenco* heels, and horse-drawn carriages were everywhere. I had a mad, crazy time; we hardly slept the entire time I was there.

Left, top to bottom: The people of Sevilla enjoying the *feria*.

Right: Even this coy young monkey, at one of the sideshows, wears the traditional polka dots.

By the time I arrived in Sevilla, the fair had been going on for a couple of days and everyone greeted me warmly. John introduced me to the woman who would be my roommate, the writer Jane Bowles. I was a bit startled. I don't know *how* Jane and her husband, Paul Bowles, looked when they left New York some years before, but in 1955 Jane was a complete hippie. She was quite a character, but a nicer roommate never lived. In his book *Engaging Eccentrics*, another old friend, the English writer David Herbert, said of her: "All Jane's works were thirty years ahead of the times. Jane's true fame came after her early death. . . . She was a perfectionist and was seldom satisfied with what she had written—alas, because of this, comparatively little of her work remains." David Herbert has lived in Tangier for many years, and for a time the Bowles lived there also. Paul Bowles wrote the introduction to David's first book, *Second Son: An Autobiography.*

Left and right, respectively: Jane; Jane with John Goodwin, both taken at the twelfth-century palace El Alcázar.

paris & rome

APRIL 25: *Returned to Madrid.*
APRIL 26: *Flew to Paris and got there in time for Charlie's birthday. Cole is still here because Paul [Sylvain] is laid up with an infected foot.*
APRIL 27: *Lunched with Cole at the Berkeley. He looks very well indeed. Paris has done him a world of good. Saw the Duchess of Windsor, Lady Diana Cooper, and Mainbocher, all lunching together. After lunch went for a drive in the park to see the flowers and tulips in the Bagatelle. Later dined with Cole, Charlie, and Christos [Bellos].*
APRIL 28: *Lunched with Cole at Coc Hardy—beautiful! Really enjoyed Cole today. He was relaxed and good company. Later had dinner with Charlie and Raoul Levy at Fouquette.*
APRIL 29: *Hair cut terribly short [for the cruise]. Spent the day in Chanel looking at clothes. Dined with Charlie at the Berkeley. Saw Irwin Shaw, Harry Kurnitz, and Arlene Francis and her husband, Martin Gable. Feeling exhausted today. Cole left for Rome. I hope to feel well enough to meet him there tomorrow.—JH*

The drive in the park was with "Miss G," Greta Garbo. She and her friend George Schlee had picked me up after lunch. After the park we went to a little shop *(left),* so she could have her watch checked, and on for a drink. She did not see Cole—she didn't want to. I was always so careful not to mention Miss G that I didn't even put this in my diary.

Right, above and below: Sir Charles Mendl.
Charlie and Marti in front of the Berkeley in Paris.

While in Paris Cole and I had lunch with his old friend Sir Charles Mendl. Later, Cole wrote to George Eells about the "strange combination of joy and sadness" that he found in Paris. The sadness lay in friends who had grown old: "For instance, I lunched with Sir Charles today. There were several young people there. And as he was helped in to lunch I realized that the guests were there because they were fond of him. He didn't know anyone was there except at rare intervals. . . . I dread old age."

APRIL 30: *Left Paris for Rome today. Sophie Litvak [Anatole's wife] came with me. She is good company. Charlie came as far as Nice, and left fighting with me. I give up! I've never known months like these past two. Dined tonight with Sturges, Cole, and Carla Boncompani. She is charming. Cocteau is here in Rome. Charming as always. After dinner drove to the fountains of Rome—beautiful night. Cole seems to love it.*
MAY 1: *May in Rome! Weather hot today. Drove to the country and lunched with Audrey Hepburn and Mel Ferrer. They seem much in love. King Vidor was there. He is going to direct* War and Peace. *Carla Boncompani with us. Dined tonight with Baroness Lo Monaco. She is wonderful company. Feel so tired.*
MAY 2: *Awakened this morning by Time, Inc. man, who said Sid James wanted me to do some pictures in Greece. Looked at dresses with Sophie Litvak. Dined tonight with Aileen Branca. Went to the opera and saw [Madame] Butterfly.*
MAY 3: *Lunched with Time, Inc. man—nice man. We talked about pictures for Greece. Cocktails at Palace Palavavici—great place. Many wonderful paintings, beautiful furniture. Princess Palavavici charming woman. Later she dined with Carla, Sturges, Cole, and me. I'd been trying on clothes all day and was exhausted.*
MAY 4: *Lunched with Aileen Branca in the flat that Ty Power bought. Dined with old gal Lillian [Baroness] Lo Monaco. She has apartment in some great palace—huge rooms—just beginning to enjoy myself when at 12 o'clock Cole wanted to go. Came back to hotel and talked to Cole until 2 A.M.! I am really dead.*
MAY 5: *Lunched with Marquessa Litta . . . charming garden, great food, first course cold rice with cold soft egg on artichoke. Went shopping with Sophie. So tired! Cocktails at another charming house—again just beginning to enjoy it when we had to go. Dined with Contessa Pecci Blunt—excellent food. We left early.*
MAY 6: *Slept late. Lunched alone. Something wrong with my kidneys. Really worried! Dined with Cole, Sturges, Eddie Condons, Marquessa Litta. To bed at 1:30 A.M.*
MAY 7: *Lunched with Cole and Carla. Tonight too sick and exhausted to go out to dinner. When this happens, Cole becomes ice . . . cold, cold ice! True, I didn't tell him until late, but it really couldn't have mattered that much.*
MAY 8: *Alone. Didn't want to lunch with anybody. Packing today. Terribly sad about Charlie. He didn't come to Rome. Instead, he is going home to California. How I wish I were with him.—JH*

I don't mean to make Cole out to be inhuman, although there were many times that I did think just that—mostly that he was inhuman toward himself. I watched him force himself to press on when it would have been far wiser to stop and rest. I tried my utmost to make him do so, but he would have none of it; he would shut me up with silence and that blank stare. And as he wouldn't complain himself, he took a very dim view of anyone else in the group who did.

Michael Pearman had sent me a clipping from Cholly Knickerbocker's March 15 column, which read: "There is absolutely no truth to those persistent rumors that Cole Porter may bring Jean Howard Feldman back from their present Mediterranean tour as his bride. Jean's only romantic attachment at the present time is her ex-husband, Charles Feldman, which is certainly not news." The clipping had been lost in my luggage for weeks. In Rome I came across it and showed it to Cole. Thinking he had some publicity person who could stop such things, I asked laughingly, "What are we going to do about this?" His reply was, "Get married!"

Left: Sturges, Cole, and I pose at the Trevi Fountains. Designed by Nicola Salvi, this was the last important Baroque work built in Rome. Legend has it, if you throw a coin over your left shoulder into this fountain, you will return to Rome.

A couple of years earlier, our mutual friends Clifton Webb, Dorothy McGuire, and Louis Jourdan had appeared in the box-office hit *Three Coins in the Fountain*, filmed here and based on the famous legend and the romantic adventures of three American girls in Rome.

Right, clockwise from top: My friend and shopping companion Sophie Litvak.

The irrepressible Baroness Lillian Lo Monaco dancing cheek to cheek with her husband at a Roman night spot.

Contessa Pecci Blunt, mother of my friend Camilla McGrath, the photographer.

Carla Boncompani and Cole in her garden near Rome.

Mel Ferrer, King Vidor, an unknown woman, and Audrey Hepburn discuss plans for the filming of *War and Peace*.

May 9: *Tired—no sleep last night, waiting for Charlie to return my call, which he did not. We talked today. Left Rome and arrived Athens—lovely soft air, like late February in Florida. Rooms pretty bad. Never have I heard noise like this—streetcars seem to come right into the room. Dined at a little place with Christos—good. Cole and Sturges on tenterhooks with each other. Funny to see Sturges dump a whole tomato and cucumber salad almost into Cole's lap.*
May 10: *Feel so bloody tired today can hardly get up. However, went out today. Lunch in a nice little place by the Aegean Sea. Finished lunch and by the time we got back to the hotel, it was six o'clock. I left the boys and went to the Acropolis to take pictures.* —JH

Sturges, who had a healthy appetite, had ordered a large green salad. As he began to eat it, Cole made some remark that he thought was funny. Apparently Sturge did not agree, because all of a sudden he stood up with fork in hand and dumped the entire thing toward Cole, just missing his lap. Cole only laughed as he brushed off a few stray salad greens. This minor contretemps did not diminish our enthusiasm for the restaurant, however, which came to be known as our "pet taverna."

Left, above and below: Five hundred feet above the streets of the city, the Acropolis, symbol of Pericles' Athenian empire, still dominates the capital.

The Parthenon (c. 447–432 B.C.), the most famous building in Greece, was dedicated to Athena the Virgin (Athena Parthenos).

Right: The west porch of the Parthenon.

MAY 11: *When I started out for dinner, I was so tired I thought I couldn't make it, but suddenly started to feel better. First time in weeks that I've felt so well. Knock. Knock. We all went to have a look at the Eros today to pick sleeping quarters. For one horrid moment I thought I would land in the dining room—but for the grace of God and Bob Bray, I would have. And if Bob does come—he may still—oh, oh! The boat is lovely. The day, however, was gray and rather cold. We eat mostly in small tavernas. Find them excellent. City of Athens clean and the people are nice.*

MAY 12: *Dead tired. Went to museum. Very, very interesting. Later, a little place on the sea for lunch. Greece, very beautiful. Later to see 5th century church—then to the Acropolis again.*

Tonight to a Mr. Sedgwick's [of the New York Times Corp.]—an American married to a Greek woman. Strange little group we made. Mad Englishman there who sang

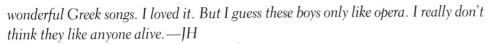

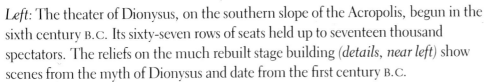

wonderful Greek songs. I loved it. But I guess these boys only like opera. I really don't think they like anyone alive.—JH

Left: The theater of Dionysus, on the southern slope of the Acropolis, begun in the sixth century B.C. Its sixty-seven rows of seats held up to seventeen thousand spectators. The reliefs on the much rebuilt stage building (*details, near left*) show scenes from the myth of Dionysus and date from the first century B.C.

Above: Cole and I leave the Hotel Grande-Bretagne, on Syntagma Square.

Right, above and below: On the same square is the national parliament building, formerly the Royal Palace.

In the forecourt, sentries (*evzones*), in traditional white uniforms, guard the memorial to the nation's unknown soldier.

Of all the treasures in the National Museum, or in all of Athens for that matter, this vibrant bronze of a boy jockey is my favorite. Found in the sea off Cape Artemision, he dates from the mid-second century B.C.

Right: About six miles west of the center of Athens, on the sacred way to Eleusis, is the Monastery of Dafni. Originally founded in the sixth century, the present building dates from the late eleventh century and is one of the finest Byzantine

structures in Greece. Pieces of sculpture from several earlier buildings can still be seen scattered about the courtyard. That's Sturges in the left foreground.

    Above: The figure of Christ Pantocrator, looking down from inside the church's dome, is the most famous of the fabulous mosaics there.

MAY 13: *And so Bob Bray is arriving [from California]. It's the dining room for me, no doubt! Dinner with George Theotoky [sent by Stavros Niarchos to play host to the Porter party during the cruise]. I went photographing today but didn't get much as the light was fading fast.*—JH

There had been some question as to whether or not Bob would be along for this part of the trip. As there was limited space, I speculated to myself that I might end up sleeping in the dining room if there were too many of us. Bob, always the perfect gentleman, took the dining room berth so I could have my own cabin.

At this point I was beginning to equate Cole's obsession with schedule and regimentation with a carefully planned military operation, and I felt like a foot soldier. Fulco di Verdura once said of Cole, "His caprices are made of steel."

It would take days of sitting around and walking around and watching it in all kinds of light to do justice to the Acropolis. It is huge but from a distance down the road, it looks small. I wanted to go back, but with this trip there often was not enough time to photograph. (The assignment for *Time* hadn't worked out because my time was not my own and I couldn't get to some of the places they wanted me to shoot.) It takes time (and solitude) to really photograph well—walking around, getting the feel of it. The light between 6:30 and 7:30 was beautiful.

Left, above and below: The Propylaia (437–432 B.C.), the monumental gatehouse to the Acropolis, caused quite a protest in ancient Athens when Pericles dipped into the city's Delion League defense fund to cover the cost of the luxurious white Pentellic marble.

The perfectly proportioned Temple of Athena Nike, bringer of victory, was completed about 427 B.C.

Right: A group of visiting schoolchildren around the Erectheion at dusk.

THE GREEK ISLANDS

ATHENS, MAY 14, 1955: *Dinner at our pet taverna, "The Old Phoenix"; then the Eros. At once a feeling of comfort and great taste.*

SUNDAY, MAY 15: *At dawn, terrific noise. Then, for breakfast, to sit on this pretty craft and look up at the Temple of Poseidon, Sunion [Cape Sounion].*—CP

Left: Cole, on deck, preparing for our visit to the Temple of Poseidon, which can just be seen in the background. On a promontory almost two hundred feet above the Saronic Sea, this temple to the mythical ruler of the sea is one of the most dramatically situated in Greece.

Above: Sturges and I take a rest at the temple. Sixteen of the original thirty-four gray-veined marble columns remain.

MONDAY, MAY 16: *Nauplia—auto-mobiles to Tiryns, Argos (theatre built out of solid rock), Mycenae (Lion's Gate), graveyards where gold masks and jewels were found, the prize of the Athens Museum, Tomb of Agamemnon (bee-hive). We set sail for Mykonos. Rough weather.—CP*

Above: One of our guides (we had three), explaining a circular enclosure that represents the early royal graveyard, dating from 1800 to 1500 B.C. It was here that Dr. Schliemann made his famous discoveries of the Mycenaean sepulchers in 1876. From left to right are Bob, Christos, George Theotoky, Sturges, Paul, Cole, and the guide.

Right: Cole being carried over the rugged pathways by Bob and Paul.

Left: Sturges and Christos leaving the
Tomb of Agamemnon, sometimes
called the Treasury of Atreus (c. 1300–
1250 B.C.). It is known as a "beehive"
tomb because of the shape of its huge,
corbeled vault.

   Above: Rough weather on our sail to
Mykonos.

TUESDAY, MAY 17: *Mykonos, a town entirely whitewashed. A donkey. I sit side-saddle and wander through enchanting streets, 360 churches here, each offered by a sailor to his saint if he would return safe from the sea, the big shock, no noise because no cars, no telephone, the ladies all weave, the gentlemen all fish, a former top whore who is now a top bootblack, bang-up lunch at a bang-up "moderne" hotel, the local museum with our delightful guide who suddenly made Greek vases interesting by explaining the progress of their decoration, the village idiot on the quai, the boat that moved in and killed our view, the constant joy of this incredible gift from Stavros.*—CP

Cole leaving the *Eros* on his special "taxi," Mike the Mule. Paul is at Cole's left, and Sturges and Bob are on his right, in the background.

Below: Fishermen bringing their boat
ashore.

    Right: Fishing nets spread on the pier
to dry in the sun.

Left: A woman weaving in her home. The weavers make beautiful skirts from these fabrics.

Below: Two fisherman relax in one of the many outdoor cafés lining the streets of the town. Most of the residents of Mykonos are seafarers.

Below: The buildings are whitewashed weekly by their owners. The entire town is spotless, dazzling white. In the moonlight the sight is unbelievably beautiful. Nearby was a charming hotel called the Leto, overlooking a good beach—the best swimming I've ever had—where for five dollars a day one could have a room with a big bath and three meals.

Right: Cole viewing the Paraportiani Church. Built on the site of an old fortress, it consists of four chapels on different levels joined to become one complex. Of the hundreds of churches on the island, this is considered the finest.

WEDNESDAY, MAY 18: *Delos. Again on a donkey, vast ruins covering acres, first the sacred part with its temples and statues, seven beautiful lions looking Syrian, phallic symbols for Temple of Dionysus, the museum with some local archaic statues, then the actual city, floors in mosaic, better mosaic than in Pompeii, a theatre holding 4,000 people. In the afternoon, Tenos with its church containing a miracle-working ikon and many gold and silver votive offerings.* —CP

Above: Cole and Christos with some of the men who rent out donkeys for the trek across Delos. Because the tour takes about three hours, most people go at least part of the way on a donkey. Riding on the back of one of these animals, however, made me much sicker than the roughest sea, and I chose to walk most of the way.

　　Right: Sturges and our guide lead the way across the island; Cole and Bob follow.

Delos, with its unbelievable navy blue sky and water, contains perhaps the most varied collection of ruins to be found in all of Greece. First settled in the third millennium B.C., this tiny island saw many changes of rule through the centuries. Its importance as a religious sanctuary was such that by 425 B.C., under the Athenians, all births, deaths, and burials were prohibited there. By 166 B.C., under Roman rule, it had become an important free port, trading in grain and, among other things, as many as ten thousand slaves daily. Former religious festivals became trade fairs, and many merchants from foreign countries began making their homes on the by-now cosmopolitan island, bringing with them vast fortunes as well as their own religions and a whole new crop of temples.

Left: One of the many headless statues that populate the island, behind which stands a temple to Isis, Egyptian goddess of fertility, built by one of the foreign merchants around the second century B.C.

Above: Cole continues the tour from atop his donkey. He rode sidesaddle because the position was more comfortable for his injured legs.

Below: Three of the nine Naxian marble sculptures (seventh century B.C.) that comprised the Terrace of the Lions still stand guard over the sacred lake where Leto, mistress of Zeus, is said to have given birth to his twin offspring— first Artemis, goddess of virginity and the hunt, and nine days later Apollo, god of truth and light.

Right: These huge marble phalli flanked the sanctuary of Dionysus (fourth century B.C.). On the base of one is a relief of a rooster (with a phallus for a head), which symbolized strength, as well as scenes from the life of this mythical god of wine and revelry.

Left: For centuries, the only inhabitants of Delos have been caretakers and their families. Here, a woman washes her clothes in the precincts of the Sacred Lake. In the background one can see the wall that circled the lake in ancient times.

Right, above and below: Sculptures from the Shrine of Bulls and Lions, symbols of strength and courage.

The day these pictures were taken, somewhere between Delos and Santorini, we were in no rush and really enjoyed the sea and the *Eros*. We even stopped so Bob could do a bit of waterskiing from the back of the Chris Craft.

Above: Cole being helped on deck by members of the crew.

Right: Sturges joins him.

Far left: Bob fishing for our lunch.

Left, top to bottom: Sturges with eyes glued to a book.
The crew clean their catch.
Lunch!
Below: Bob with *his* catch.
Right: George, Cole, Sturges, and Bob being silly at
dinner. Of all the appointments afforded us on the *Eros*, this
crazy table fascinated everyone because it was balanced in
such a way that no matter how rough the weather or how far
to one side the boat tipped, the food and dishes stayed exactly
where they had been placed. Christos was not as lucky. After
a few days of rough weather he had to leave us; he was green
in the face from seasickness. We didn't see him again until we
returned to Athens.

THURSDAY, MAY 19: *Santorini (Venetian name), Thira (Greek
name). In port beside an unreachable cliff. Then all of us on
donkeys by triangular zig-zag pavements to the summit to find
not only a fairy-tale town with fascinating vistas in every street
but also a view down to the sea on the other side, everything
green and accessible and, as against the cliffside, strangely
uninhabited. The museum with two Egyptian torsos and a
lovely fresco from Crete. Then a visit to the Vulcan hotel to
meet the proprietress, who gave us local wine and cakes and
exhausting French truisms. Down by donkey to harbor to
board the Chris Craft to examine a nearby volcanic island,
which rose from the sea only in the early 1920s. As we skirted
the shores of this already cool mass of lava, I felt the beginnings
of the earth and the terrors of hell.*

FRIDAY, MAY 20: *A shock to wake up in the harbor of Rhodes to see on the left a big medieval chateau fort, on the right a church that recalled the church in Verona and a campanile, in front of us a Turkish-looking building and in the background, infinite greenery. Later, in motors, first to the Hospital of the Knights of St. John and its museums, then through the Street of the Knights to the Palace of the Great Masters (mosaics from island of Kos), surrounded by three rows of outer walls with two moats. In the evening, folk dances in the public square. Greek airmen in uniform suddenly joined the girl dancers in their traditional costumes and the contrast of today and long-ago was touching.*

SATURDAY, MAY 21: *Rhodes. By car to the top of Mount Philerimos, next to ruins at Kamiros (2nd century B.C.), then to Valley of Butterflies for a big lunch by a brook. Afterwards, nap and tea at Hotel des Roses.*

SUNDAY, MAY 22: *Motored to Lindos. Arrived to find remnants of the fourth century B.C. and a vast medieval castle on top of a great hill by the sea. Terrific heat so we all decide not to make the trip. Good lunch in a cool restaurant. Nearby a table of Americans, the men drinking quantities of martinis and straight whiskeys. They decided not to make the climb either. The blessed Eros rounded the point and we boarded her to find a cool breeze.* —CP

A kidney infection finally knocked me down at Lindos. I had a raging fever of 104–5, and a very fine Greek doctor appeared and saved my life. Bob Bray was watchful and kind to me during the fever. He would change the sheets, which were dripping wet, many times during the days and nights.
Left: The Valley of the Butterflies gets its name from the hundreds of thousands of Quadrina butterflies that arrive annually in order to mate. They are attracted by the vanilla-scented resin of the valley's storax trees.

Right: At Lindos, the ruins of the temple to Athena Lindos, patron goddess of the city, are visible among fortress ruins.

MONDAY, MAY 23: *A glorious morning, whitecaps and the* Eros *under full sail. Heraclion, Crete. Left late afternoon, motored to Phaestos, countryside very hilly and fertile. Ruins at Phaestos disappointing what with only the foundations left to see.* —CP

In mythology, Crete is, among other things, home of the famous minotaur —the monstrous offspring of King Minos's wife Pasiphae and the beautiful white sacrificial bull given to the king by Poseidon—which the king hid in the legendary labyrinth of Knossos. In reality, Crete is believed to have been inhabited as early as 6000 B.C. and has had many foreign rulers through the centuries, including the Dorians, the Romans, the Saracen Arabs, the Genoese, the Venetians, and the Ottomans. In 1913 Crete became part of Greece but retains a fiercely independent spirit. Modern inhabitants have been known to refer to Crete as a continent.

Left: An elderly Cretan crossing a street in Heraclion.

Right: The rich countryside of Crete is scattered with farms and vineyards.

TUESDAY, MAY 24: *Heraclion, Crete. Motored to Knossos. Great ruins of palace partially and excellently restored. Then to museum at Heraclion; fascinating treasures, golden and precious stone jewels, jar sculptures and frescoes in many colors. The high spots—a sculptured bull's head and a profile fresco of a very dressy lady with painted lips known as "La Parisienne."—CP*

About three miles from Heraclion, Knossos, with its Royal Palace of King Minos, was the earliest capital of Crete. The palace was occupied from about 2000 to 1400 B.C., during

which time it was destroyed several times (supposedly by earthquakes) and rebuilt. The present ruins represent the appearance of the complex around 1600 B.C.

Left: The north gateway of the palace gives a good idea of the unusual and beautiful architecture with its columns that widen at the top.

Above left: Bronze Age storage jars (*pithoi*), tall as a person, were used to keep the enormous amounts of grain, oil, wine, and other provisions necessary for a population that at one time may have numbered as many as 100,000 citizens.

Above right: A portion of a surviving exterior fresco of a captive bull.

Left: Cole, with his guide in attendance, sits upon what is traditionally called the throne of King Minos. Carved of gypsum, it might instead have been the ritual chair of the

high priestess known as the Lady of the Labyrinth.

    Above: One of two wingless griffins that sit among lilies and face the throne from opposite sides.

Above: The elegant "Blue Ladies" fresco.

Right: Found at the Little Palace, this sacrificial vessel *(rhyton)* in the form of a bull's head is made of black steatite and inlaid with limestone, jasper, and mother-of-pearl. The eyes are of rock crystal.

It's really a miracle this picture turned out. Photographs weren't allowed and I was shooting through glass without much light or a flash. It took quite a long exposure with only the camera strap around my neck to help hold it steady.

WEDNESDAY, MAY 25: *En route to Katacolon, port near Olympia. A wonderful day, brisk day, jib and foresail up. In late A.M. passed Cythera where Aphrodite was born, then up west coast of Peloponnesus.* —CP

Thursday, May 26: Katacolon. Short drive to Olympia. We went all over the ruins, the most notable feature, the great size of the sections of the columns of the Temple of Zeus. In the museum, the east and west pediments of this temple and the Hermes of Praxiteles in Parian marble.—CP

It was Hercules himself, the ancients claimed, who chose this spot in the luxuriant Alfios valley for the sacred games that were the predecessors of the modern Olympics. As early as the tenth century B.C., altars were erected to Hera and Zeus among the groves of plane, poplar, oak, pine, and wild olive trees.

Clockwise from lower left: Among enormous fallen columns, the group makes its way. Cole is in his wheelchair; Paul and George are behind him; Bob (pushing Cole) talks to the guide, who is almost completely hidden; and Sturges surveys the sights.

Rows of column drums from the Temple of Zeus (470–456 B.C.), which once held Phidias's colossal statue of the god. Almost as large as the Parthenon, it is believed to have been toppled by a series of earthquakes.

This Roman arch covers the stone passageway that is the main entrance to the third of the three Olympic stadiums built here.

Praxiteles' Hermes (350–330 B.C), in the Olympia Museum, is an example of Greek sculpture at its height.

Friday, May 27: *Itea (port near Delphi). Cars up into the hills passing through groves of olive trees. The museum with friezes from Temple of Apollo and bronze charioteer. Then a hard donkey ride to site of the oracle and the surrounding ruins, a wonderful view, very melodramatic.*

Off across the gulf, arriving evening at port of Corinth. —CP

Legend has it that Apollo's father, Zeus, freed two eagles at opposite ends of the world and determined that the point at which they crossed in flight—Delphi, home of Apollo and Dionysus—would represent the center of the universe.

The ancient Greeks' most important sanctuary, Delphi is located on the slopes of Mount Parnassus between two soaring crags, the Phaedriades, two thousand feet above the Gulf of Corinth.

Left: Three local gentlemen watch our group preparing to begin the tour. Left to right are Sturges, Paul (with Cole's wheelchair), George, Cole, and Bob.

Above: An old peasant woman guarding her donkey. Behind her is a theater built in the fourth century B.C. and enlarged by the Romans to seat five thousand spectators on limestone terraces.

Below: Two youths stare at each other across the centuries as they await installation at the Delphi Museum. On the left is Antinous (the favorite of the Roman emperor Hadrian) portrayed as Apollo (c. A.D. 130–35). The soft modeling and relaxed pose are characteristic of the romantic sensibility of the Hadrianic period. To his left is one of the twins Cleobis and Biton, sculpted by Polymedes of Argos (c. 615–590 B.C.), whose rigid, frontal stance exemplifies archaic Greek sculpture.

Right: The Temple of Apollo (c. 330 B.C.), the heart of the sanctuary at Delphi, housed the god's famous oracle.

Far right: The Delphi Museum's finest treasure is this charioteer (470 B.C.), one of only half a dozen bronzes surviving from the classical Greek era. The winner's ribbon around his head is inlaid with silver. The eyes are made of white enamel, bronze, and black onyx, with copper lips and eyebrows and tiny copper wire lashes.

SATURDAY, MAY 28: *By car to museum. Corinthian vases whose decoration shows strong oriental influence. Temple of Zeus [Apollo], 700 B.C., a few columns standing, then the ruins of a big agora. Far above us, on a great hill, the* Acrocorinth, *where the prostitutes lived in the days of Corinth's glory. In the afternoon, through the Corinth Canal, arriving in the evening at Epidaurus.* SUNDAY, MAY 29: *Drove to theatre, 350 B.C., holding 15,000 people.*—CP

Left: The *Eros*, though not a large boat, still was an uncomfortably close fit as we made our way through the Corinth canal, which is almost four miles long but only eighty-two feet wide and twenty-six feet deep. Begun by the French in 1882, the canal was finished by the Greeks in 1893.

Right: Sturges and Bob at the magnificent theater of Epidaurus, attributed to Polyclitus the Younger, who applied intricate mathematical formulas to create ideal sight lines and near-perfect acoustics. The original theater (400 B.C.) had thirty-four rows of seats; two hundred years later twenty-one rows were added.

Monday May 30. Aegina. A car to the temple of Aphaea on the top of the island in its very center, looking over the sea on every side. To Piraeus after lunch aboard with toasts from & to the crew. The dream is over.

After the cruise we returned to Athens, where we stayed two or three days. Cole and Sturge then left for Switzerland and I left for Rome, where I met Marti. We stayed in Rome about four days and then went on to Zurich for four or five days. I left for New York on June 10 and Marti went to London.

Top: Cole's diary entry for the last day of our cruise, written in one of his music notebooks.

Above: Cole, Sturges, and I opened and closed the Greek trip at our "pet taverna," the Old Phoenix, located in Piraeus, a suburb of Athens.

Right: Christos, Sturges, and Cole back at the Old Phoenix after the cruise.

Cole and Sturges on camels.
Sturges, Linda, and Cole in the Temple of Amon at Karnak.

Early in 1921 Cole, Linda, Sturges, and Martha Hyde journeyed to Egypt.
While there they visited the diggings of Howard Carter, courtesy of an introduction
from Carter's partner and Linda's friend, Lord Carnarvon. The dig would
result in the discovery of the tomb of King Tut the following year.

In her photograph album, Linda captioned this picture,
taken at Deir al-Bahri, "Cole being dreadful."

i LOVED THE GREEK ISLANDS, especially Crete, and hoped
to return some day. We all had managed without too much
effort to get along with each other in close quarters—happily.

By July Cole and I were both back in California—he
working on the film score for *High Society*, I busy developing
and printing film from our trip.

On July 4th we both attended Joe Cotten's memorable
Independence Day luncheon party. Cole was happy and
feeling well, as indeed was I—of course our recent travels
were a topic of conversation that day. Just as I had suggested
the first journey, Cole suddenly said, "Let's do it again!" I
laughed and replied, "Why not?" That started the ball rolling.

Having committed myself, I knew that I had to have
someone to talk to this time and was determined to have
Marti Stevens come *with* us on this trip. I had known Marti
for many years. She was a perfect traveling companion,
energetic, bright as sunshine, and she could always make me
laugh—as she does to this day. I told Cole this and he replied
that she would need a passport and I should show her the
itinerary so she could buy her tickets. It was never discussed
again. It seemed odd to me that it hadn't occurred to Cole
that, just as he had had Bob and Sturges on the first trip, I
might need someone of my own sex along for company on
such a long journey.

Howard Sturges died of a heart attack in October of 1955 in
Paris. Because he died so suddenly, with no advance warning
or illness, in some ways his death was a greater shock to Cole
than those of Cole's mother and his beloved Linda.

As was his way, Cole simply went on, and in February our
second journey began. Cole again invited Robert Bray, who
joined us for extended portions of the trip. We would begin
again from Switzerland and make stops again in Rome,
Monte Carlo, and Athens; however, this time we would visit
different places along the way in Italy (especially Sicily) and
France, also in Spain, where we would spend quite a bit more
time, skipping Portugal and adding Egypt and the Middle
East. Stavros Niarchos had again offered the *Eros II* for our
cruise to many of the Greek islands we had not seen the
year before.

Collier Young and Cole sipping mint
juleps at Joe Cotten's Fourth of July party, 1955.

THE SECOND TRIP 1956

FROM: COLE PORTER

September 19, 1955

Dearest Jeannie:
     When I talked to you on the telephone the
beautiful album of our Greek cruise had not yet
arrived. You say that this is not a work of art, but
to me it definitely is and I shall always treasure it!
     I miss you dreadfully.
     My love to you both.
                              Cole

A note from Cole following the
first trip.

FEBRUARY 29, 1956: *Flew from St. Moritz to Madrid in Niarchos' DC3, a four-and-a-half-hour flight. Spring!* —CP

By February 29 we had been in St. Moritz for about ten days. As always, we attended many parties, which may be the reason I can't remember the theme of this one, given by Eugenie and Stavros Niarchos at Chesa Veglia, or the reason all the girls are wearing matching shirts.

Left, top to bottom: Marina Cicogna and I enter the room beneath crossed swords. The gentleman to my left is Count Theo Rossi di Montelera, who appears to be dressed as Don Quixote . . . could this be a clue to the theme?

Holding hands, at top, are Eugenie Niarchos and Cristina Agnelli Brandolini d'Adda. In the center, left to right, are Eliane Page, Wynn de L'Espée, Geneviève de Caumont, Madame La Force, Marina Cicogna, Muriel Bing, and a girl with so much metallic makeup that I can't tell who she is. In the front row are Noel Salinas, me, Idette Liechti, Teresa (Terry) von Pantz, Claire Clémence de Maille, and Elise Hunt.

The girls take Theo in hand.

Right, top to bottom: There I am in the center, with Bebino Salinas and Muriel Bing.

A forgotten face with Christos Bellos and Marina Cicogna.

Paulette Goddard navigates the room

Far right, above and below: Wynn and Stavros have appropriated Theo's hat and take turns wearing it for the camera.

113

spain

MARCH 1: *Dined with Albas in completely restored Palacio de Liria.*
MARCH 2: *Arrived Cordova.*
MARCH 3: *Cordova Mosque. Afternoon, arrived Sevilla.*—CP

The "Albas" Cole refers to are the Duke and Duchess of Alba. Of all Linda's suitors before her marriage to Cole, the duke was probably the most serious. Everyone assumed they would pursue a morganatic marriage, but the Catholic church forbade the union because of Linda's divorce. The Palacio de Liria is the magnificent eighteenth-century palace the Albas called home. It now contains a museum displaying the family's priceless collections of art and furnishings.

Left: The red-and-white-striped double arches of the Great Mosque of Cordova (La Mezquita). Begun in 785 by Abd-er-Rahman I, the building was claimed by the Christians in 1236.

Right: Looking down a delightful Morisco-style Cordova street—the tower of the mosque can be seen in the distance. In the sixteenth century, the Holy Roman Emperor Charles V authorized the building of a "proper" cathedral within the mosque and the rebuilding of its minaret into a bell tower.

MARCH 4: *Sevilla, El Alcázar.*
MARCH 5: *Sevilla Cathedral. At 7:00 P.M., a concert in my honor at orphanage—boys seven to fourteen, singing sacred and regional songs. Expert singing and touching experience.*
MARCH 6: *Left Sevilla. At 1:00 P.M. arrived Jerez de la Frontera. To Gonzales-Biass sherry winery. A lot of local students there in choirboy robes, the robes trimmed in long ribbons, each from a different girl. They elected Jean Howard their "queen", then they all took off their robes to make a beautifully soft dance floor. Surrounding Jean in a circle, they persuaded her to dance on their robes as they sang and played their mandolins and guitars. Jean became suddenly Spanish and danced like a lovely gypsy. Arrived Algeciras at 7:00 P.M. Hotel Reina Cristina. A strange kick to look out the window and see the Rock of Gibraltar—and an unexpected shock to find a hot-coal fire in my sitting room after dinner, arranged by Robert. Nice surprise!*
MARCH 7: *Lunch at Hotel Rock, Gibraltar. Gibraltar so big and so British. In the late afternoon, Fuengirola on the Mediterranean. Hotel Malhamar. Customers here mostly British and Scandinavian. The British have been coming to this Costa del Sol for years. Thus, dull food as against the rest of Spain. . . . Hotel run by a brilliant young Spanish girl. "Papa always in Madrid." She could run the Chase National Bank.*—CP

Left: Cole looking at a statue of Mercury at the center of an enormous lily pond in the Alcázar Gardens. The pink stone wall beyond, with its recessed frescoes, was built by Charles V.

Right: Three gentlemen of Sevilla.

Above: Bob Bray with Cole's Cadillac, license plate CP–11.

Right: Cole with one of his ever-present guidebooks, on the ferry to Jerez de la Frontera.

MARCH 8: *Drive to lunch to Ronda–remarkable bridge and house of the Moorish king.—CP*

The Casa del Rey Moro (House of the Moorish King) takes its name from a tiled portrait on its outside wall. Now a private residence, legend says it was once the home of King Badis, a Moorish ruler who drank wine from the jewel-encrusted skulls of his victims. In reality, it is only about two hundred years old.

Left: Cole, with our guide, looking out over El Taja, the famous four-hundred-foot gorge created by the Guadalevín River, which literally divides Ronda in two.

Above: One of three bridges that span El Taja.

Ronda is celebrated as the birthplace of bullfighting in the classic style. Over generations, a local family, the Romeros, developed most of the rules and techniques—including the introduction of the cape—still used today.

Below: Bob substitutes his jacket and takes the matador's

stance on the oldest bullring site in Spain. The current structure, the Corrida Goyesca, was built in 1785 on the site of an earlier ring.

Left: Bob's audience, a lone black cat, sits among the numbered seats.

MARCH 9: *Evening, Granada. Alhambra Palace Hotel, after driving through beautiful mountains covered with blooming fruit trees. The road wonderful.*

MARCH 10: *The Alhambra. At night a great gypsy song-and-dance show in a cave.*—CP

The name Alhambra is applied to a whole group of buildings within and around this walled enclosure. The word is from the Arabic *kalahamra*, which means red castle, a reference to the color of the iron-rich mud used for the bricks from which its walls are made.

Left: Two local policemen pose with me at a crossroads upon our arrival at Granada.

Right, above and below: The cultivated countryside, a corner of the Alhambra wall, and Granada beyond.

At the Alhambra, both the Palacio de los Leons (Palace of the Lions) and, within the palace, the Patio de los Leons (Court of the Lions) take their names from this fountain. Its basin is supported by twelve gray marble beasts that are much earlier than the fourteenth-century home of Muhammad V, in which the fountain is situated. At one time water flowed from the mouth of a different lion each hour of the day, was caught in the four slender channels that crisscross the floor, and was carried into every part of the palace for household use.

MARCH 11: *The Royal Chapel with the tombs of Ferdinand and Isabella, Joanna the Mad, and Philip the Fair.*
MARCH 12: *The Generalife.* —CP

Below: For centuries Granada's main gypsy quarter, called Scaromonte, has been located on a hill above the Alhambra. Many of the people of this area still live in what appeared to be comfortable caves and make a habit of inviting visitors in for

flamenco music and dancing and vastly overpriced wine—at the visitors' expense. In such a cave are Paul, our guide, Cole, me, and Marti, with our hosts.

   Right: Also above the Alhambra proper, but considered a part of it, is the Generalife (pronounced hay-nay-rah-lee-fay); derived from Arabic, it translates as "Garden of the Architect." A simple white palace with pavilions, it was the summer home of the Nasrid rulers. Its most charming feature is the Patio de la Acequina (Patio of the Canal), a paradise rich with plants—down its center is a long, narrow pool with fountain jets creating arches of sparkling water from either side.

While in Monte Carlo, Cole dined with his friends Pierre and Charlotte de Monaco, parents of Prince Ranier. Within months the prince would meet Grace Kelly, there to film *To Catch a Thief.*

Above: The view from my room at the Hotel de Paris in Monte Carlo.

Right: Our arrival at Palermo. Cole and Marti head for the car, which Luigi had brought ahead to meet us.

Later, while driving through Palermo, Luigi turned the car into a rather narrow street—it got more and more narrow the farther we went. Finally it got so narrow we couldn't move at all—a horse had to be brought to pull us out backward!

monaco & italy

MARCH 26: *Monday. La Favorita, charming Chinese royal villa; Capella Palatina; Bagheria, Palagonia villa with monster statues, tombs of Norman and Hohenstaufen royalties in cathedral.* —CP

Left: The little town of Bagheria is known for its collection of Baroque villas, of which the Villa Palagonia is the most intriguing. A truly extravagant folly, the exterior is decorated with sixty-two statues of half-human, half-animal creatures. Built in 1715 by architect Thomas Maria Napoli for Francesco Gravina, a prince of Palagonia, the army of grotesques was almost immediately blamed for the birth of several "living monsters" in the village, and pregnant women were discouraged from visiting the villa and its precincts.

Right, above and below: Marti leaving the Villa la Favorita, built in the chinoiserie style (the little palace is often called Palazzina Cinese) by Queen Maria Carolina as a diversion during husband Ferdinand IV's first exile from Naples in 1799.

The town of Monreale (five miles southwest of Palermo) grew up around and during the building of King William the Good's cathedral from 1172 to 1189. In this picture I am standing near the Arabic fountain in a corner of the cloister in the Benedictine monastery that joins the south side of the chapel. Like the whole of this wondrous place, this arcaded cloister is richly decorated; 25 arches are supported by 216 columns—set in pairs, alternating plain and ornate—each topped with a unique and elaborately carved capital.

The procession at Agrigento continues.

Left: I am standing before the Cathedral of Syracuse (Santa Maria delle Colonne). With its Sicilian Baroque facade by Andrea Palma, it appears to be a typical eighteenth-century church. However, it is really a Christian church literally infesting a still-existing ancient Greek temple to Athena (480 B.C.). Over the centuries it has been added to and altered in the Byzantine, Norman, Gothic, and Baroque styles. Somewhere between a historical marvel and an architectural nightmare, it is certainly amazing.

Right: Cole and I take a break in Syracuse.

APRIL 1: *The Ear of Dionysius, Greek theatre, Roman theatre.*
APRIL 2: *Easter Monday. Drove through laughing crowds to Hotel San Domenico, Taormina.*
APRIL 3: *Roman (Graeco-Roman) theatre, drive way up to the village Castel Mola; later, Public Gardens.* —CP

Below: Marti at the Ear of Dionysius. North of modern Syracuse, the Latomie caves, where the original city's stone was quarried, are now planted as gardens. In ancient times the tyrant Dionysius is said to have thrown uncommunicative prisoners into one of these caves, the entrance of which is shaped like a huge ear. Because of the cave's excellent

acoustical properties, he could listen to their conversations and gain the information he was unable to torture from them.

Right: Extraordinary acoustics are also to be found at the theater at Taormina. D. H. Lawrence had always been one of my favorite writers, and I was really looking forward to seeing a place where he had lived and that he had written about. From the moment we arrived, the skies opened and the rains began. The whole time we were there, it either rained or the fog was so heavy little could be seen. This photograph shows the A.D. 300 Roman addition to the 300 B.C. Greek theater. The fog obscured the spectacular view of Mount Etna in the distance.

APRIL 4: *Rest and clean.*
APRIL 5: *From Messina by boat to Cosenza. Calabria lovely, mountainous but fertile country. All peasant women in bright red skirts with black bustles.*
APRIL 6: *Into Apulia in the rain. Picnic lunch in the car. Taranto.*
APRIL 7: *Drove through strange Trulli region. Trulli are cone-shaped stone houses with white tops and curious designs on their fronts. Drove through terrible hailstorm, arriving for lunch, Bari—bitter cold and awful wind. In P.M. saw*

Cathedral of San Nicolas and San Gregorio, also Frederick II castle.—CP

Above: Cole in the comfort of his "Caddie" as the ferry makes its way from Messina to Cosenza.

Right: Marti before examples of Apulia's vernacular architecture. The *trulli* are circular one-room peasant homes built of stone with a simple hole in the roof to let smoke escape. This form has survived almost unchanged since the second millennium B.C. and still serves the inhabitants well.

APRIL 8: *Sunday. Still bitter cold. Molfetta, Duomo Vecchio; . . . Trani, beautiful Romanesque cathedral, lunch, then [to] Barletta, San Sepolcro (thirteenth century), nearby ugly Colossus of* A.D. *fourth century. Motored by battlefield of Cannae where Hannibal defeated Romans in 216* B.C. *Castel del Monte, magnificent, thirteenth century. Castle of Frederick II on hilltop. The whole countryside nearly covered with snow. We found a nearby bar and drank coffee and homemade liqueurs. Back to Bari, still so cold, and the cyclonic wind goes on.*—CP

Left: Here I am shivering, but smiling, before the Castel del Monte (1240)—the largest and favorite of several Norman castles built in this area by Frederick II. With its eight beautifully restored, eight-sided towers, it commands one of the best views in southern Italy and has been compared to the Colosseum for "splendor and significance."

Right, above and below: Marti makes a less detailed inspection than the little girl at the knees of this bronze colossus, which stands before Chiesa del San Sepolcro. The figure is thought to be of a Byzantine emperor, perhaps Valentinian. The church is a composite of Romanesque, Norman, Gothic, and Renaissance styles.

Paul, Luigi, and I warm up while sampling the local liqueurs.

APRIL 9: *Drove over Apennine mountains to Naples and warm sunshine. The dear Hotel Excelsior, a beautiful suite overlooking the bay. Henry May waiting in the bar.*
APRIL 10: *Pompeii.*
APRIL 11: *The great palace of Caserta, beautiful architecture, fountains, and gardens. Also, fascinating eighteenth-century and Napoleonic (Murat) interiors. In the evening to San Carlo to hear* Gugliemo Tell [William Tell]. *Tebaldi magnificent but the opera a dud. Museo della Floridiana—porcelain.*
APRIL 12: *Posillipo.*
APRIL 13: *Rest and clean.*
APRIL 14: *National Museum—frescoes, mosaics, and sculptures from Pompeii and Herculaneum. Also frescoes from Paestum.*
APRIL 15: *Sunday. Church and Museo di San Martino.*—CP

It was in Naples that Cole finally lost his temper over Marti's tardiness. Marti was never late when it really mattered, but at times when, after motoring all day, she wanted to linger in a nice warm bath a bit longer, she couldn't see the harm in being just a minute late for the 8:15 meeting at the bar before dinner.

But to Cole it mattered a lot. I have seen him go into dinner, leaving whoever might be late to walk in to the dinner table alone, red-faced with embarrassment. This night, when Marti and I came downstairs, not more than ten minutes late, Cole was not in the bar—he was at the concierge's desk. He turned to Marti and began to pound his cane on the floor, shouting, "You're *always* late . . . you destroy any trip!" He absolutely exploded. Needless to say, everyone was right on time for the rest of the trip.

Left: On the afternoon of August 24, A.D. 79, time was stopped here at Pompeii by an eruption of Mount Vesuvius. I am standing near the Macellum (provisions market) at the east side of the Forum. This area is the most important example of a Roman civic center known. Behind the colonnade were the shops of the *argentari* (money changers); the pilasters were once bases for statues. In 1749, when the first bronzes and marbles were discovered by workmen digging along the Sarno canal about fifteen miles from Naples, the ancient artifacts began to revolutionize the taste of Europe. Pompeii immediately became a "must see" on everyone's grand tour.

Right: The large theater at Pompeii (second century B.C.) predates the oldest permanent theater in Rome and held about five thousand people. The portico behind was remodeled during Nero's reign to make a barracks, armory, and lockup for the gladiators who performed here.

EGYPT

APRIL 16–19: *Rome, hectic.*
APRIL 20: *Seven-hour flight to Cairo and Mena House.* —CP

The Mena House is a charming Edwardian-type hotel near Cairo. Cole arranged for our rooms to look out upon the changing light of the Sahara. The effect was beautiful.

Below: Cole, Marti, and I discuss the next day's itinerary with one of our guides at the Mena House. The hotel was originally built as a royal hunting lodge. It was

gradually enlarged and in 1869 converted into a guest house for the gala opening of the Suez Canal. When we visited, one could still sit on the famous veranda and sip tea or cocktails with a magical undisturbed view of the Great Pyramids. This was of course before the paved road up to the pyramids added a stream of cars and buses to the view.

Right: Marti and I step (or should I say ride) into a postcard view before one of the Great Pyramids. The ruins immediately around us are of the old cemetery, part of an enormous funerary complex, of which the Great Pyramids were the focal point.

APRIL 21: *Saturday. Cairo. Pyramids, Sphinx, Mosque of Sultan Hassan, Mosque of Mohammad Ali (all alabaster).*—CP

Below: The Great Pyramids are the only surviving example of the Seven Wonders of the Ancient World. These royal tombs were built (in order of descending size) by: Cheops, c. 2690 B.C.; Cheophren, c. 2650 B.C.; and Menkaru, c. 2600 B.C. Romanticized almost to the point of boredom (one guidebook says, "From a distance

they look like the world's largest paperweights"), in almost five thousand years of prose, poetry, song, art, and photography, it is only when you actually stand before them that their full impact is realized.

Left: Almost as famous as the Great Pyramids, and lying only about 500 feet away, is the Sphinx. With the body of a lion (representing kingship and might) and the head of a human (representing intelligence), it faces east to watch the rising of the sun and with it the return of life each day. Carved out of a single piece of living stone, it measures 190 feet in length and is known as *Abu'l-Hul*, or Father of Terror.

155

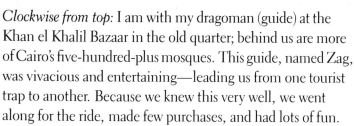

Clockwise from top: I am with my dragoman (guide) at the Khan el Khalil Bazaar in the old quarter; behind us are more of Cairo's five-hundred-plus mosques. This guide, named Zag, was vivacious and entertaining—leading us from one tourist trap to another. Because we knew this very well, we went along for the ride, made few purchases, and had lots of fun.

The interior of the Mosque of Mohammad Ali, with its chandeliers made of enormous rings suspended from the ceiling is hung with dozens of illuminated crystal balls.

Before entering a mosque all must remove their shoes. An alternative offered at many mosques is to rent funny, baglike shoe covers like the ones I am shown stepping into at the entrance of the Mosque of Mohammad Ali.

The Mosque of Sultan Hassan (c. 1356–63) is built in the shape of a cross; at its center is this beautiful fountain. The largest mosque in Cairo, it is a masterpiece of Islamic architecture.

APRIL 22: *Sunday. Memphis and its lying-down Colossus. Sakkara, the great underground tombs of the sacred bulls, the step pyramid earlier than all.*—CP

Memphis (about twenty miles southwest of Cairo, across the Nile) was one of the greatest cities of the ancient world and the first capital of unified Egypt. At its height, the city held half a million people; today its brick houses have returned to mud. Most of the stone monuments were used as construction materials when Muslim conquerors moved their capital to Cairo.

Opposite, clockwise from far left: Local women and children at the little village of Mit-Rahine, where the only two important artifacts of Memphis are now preserved.

One of these is this alabaster sphinx, which is probably from the entrance to the Temple of Ptah.

The second, and more impressive, is this huge colossus of Ramses II, also carved in alabaster. Ramses littered Egypt with similar outsize likenesses of himself, and is known as the greatest monument builder of all time.

Right, top to bottom: One of our camel drivers in front of a step pyramid. The shape is thought to represent the stairway to heaven, as opposed to the later flat-sided pyramids, which are thought to represent shafts of sunlight descending from the clouds. Also unlike later pyramids, these do not actually contain burial chambers but are solid throughout and are built as landmarks over underground tombs.

A local farmer drawing water from an ancient well.

Of all the guides we had on these journeys—and we had a lot, sometimes as many as three at a time—this gentleman was my favorite: a beautiful man.

APRIL 23: *The Cairo Museum, the early Egypt, the middle and the late—the late beginning with Akhenaton, then to Tutankhamen and incredible loot from Tutankhamen's tomb in Luxor, discovered in 1922 by Carnarvon and Howard Carter. Everything in top condition and of extreme beauty.*—CP

Below, left and right: This portrait statue of Cheophren, carved in diorite, was one of a series made for his funerary temple near the Sphinx. The falcon,

symbol of the sun, protectively enfolding his head designates him the son of Re (Ra).

The King's Mannequin, carved in wood, gessoed, and painted. This exactly life-size figure of Tut was used to fit his jewelry and robes.

Right: Prince Rahotep and his wife Nofret in painted limestone (c. 2610 B.C.) are among the few examples of this type of lifelike sculptures left completely intact. The portrait faces are further enlivened by quartz eyes.

APRIL 24: *For dinner, a beautiful tent in the desert, under the full moon. We looked at the pyramids from the opposite side and the light on them was enchanting. After dinner, an Arab orchestra, two belly dancers, two male Sudanese comedians, and a beautiful Arabian horse, the only horse I have ever seen who could dance, even without his rider, in perfect tempo. On the way home, the usual stop to look at the Sphinx who has been there watching for five thousand years.*
APRIL 25: *Back to the Museum.* —CP

Cole didn't tell me the details of our dinner in the desert in advance, and I was not prepared to take pictures. It was naughty of him—the evening was beautiful and would have made for beautiful pictures.

Cairo has one of the great museums of the world. I felt I needed more time to get the pictures I wanted. I discussed this with Marti, saying that I simply didn't know how to get around Cole. In the end, I had to lie to him. Early the next morning before Cole was up, we called Paul's room and Marti did the talking. She told him that I was ill with a high fever and could not leave as planned—that we would fly to meet them in Beirut. With special permission I spent the entire day getting all the pictures I wanted.

Left: Of the more than three thousand pieces in the Tut collection, this mask, which covered the face of the mummy, may be the most beautiful— it is certainly the best known. Made of solid gold, the headdress is inlaid with strips of blue glass, the eyelids with lapis lazuli, and the necklace with a combination of colored glass and precious stones. On the forehead of the boy king (he ruled from the age of nine, dying at the age of nineteen in 1324 B.C.) are the vulture and *vraeus*, representing the gods of Upper and Lower Egypt.

Below: Another evening, I had it in mind to somehow take an unusual picture of this much photographed ruin. I decided to do it by moonlight. This brilliant idea didn't last long. Finally it was Cole who thought to pay local children to build bonfires below

the Sphinx's majestic face for added light. We were both quite pleased with our combined effort. Today you can't get near the Sphinx after closing time, much less build a fire—you'd have the entire Egyptian army on you.

LeBanon

APRIL 27: *Friday. By plane to Beirut, Lebanon. Hotel Excelsior, excellent. Beirut beautiful and as against Cairo, not even one fly.*

APRIL 29: *Sunday. Drove to Byblos and saw ruins of so many civilizations, unluckily not beautiful. Up through magnificent country to a sad little patch of Lebanon cedars, some of them very old. The night in Tripoli, a run-down*

town. The hotel a remnant of Turkish domination. Terrible cozy corners but bang-up food.

APRIL 30: *To the Krak des Chevaliers, a magnificent fortress originally built by the Kurds and later enlarged to become the finest example of what the crusaders could build. It is on top of a mountain and looks like a big walled city. Once inside, one goes up and up on a rather*

wide road designed for horsemen, until finally the summit.

I was carried up and then down by Paul, the Lebanese guide, and the two chauffeurs. They were exhausted and I felt sorry for them. But the Krak (Turkish for fortress) is one of the world's greatest wonders.

On to Baalbek and the charming Hotel Palmyra, with its delightful patron and patroness.

MAY 1: *Tuesday. In the morning to the most beautiful Roman ruins, the Temple of Jupiter with its very high columns, the Temple of Bacchus, on a smaller scale but nearly complete. Great restoration is being done here. A glimpse at the Temple of Venus, very little left. On to Damascus, seeing only the new city, to the Hotel Omayyad.*—CP

The name *baal* dates back as far as 1700 B.C. and is believed to be the name used for the presiding god of a given locality rather than a specific entity. The ancient Greeks called Baalbek Heliopolis, "City of the Sun." The ruins were described by Robert Wood as "the remains of the boldest plan we ever saw attempted in architecture."

Left: Only six of the original fifty-four columns of the Temple of Jupiter (c. A.D. 60) remain standing. They are a monumental fifty-four feet high and seven feet in diameter.

Right: Nearby, the Temple of Bacchus (c. A.D. 150–200) is much smaller than its neighbor but still *larger* than the Parthenon. One of the most highly decorated of all temples, it was converted into a Christian church by Emperor Theodosius at the end of the fourth century. It is raised on a massive substructure containing some of the largest single blocks of stone in the world. The city was destroyed by earthquakes in 1795, and the German government began excavation here in 1902

syria

MAY 2: *Damascus. St. Paul's window from which he escaped, Ananias's house, underground (now a chapel), where he hid before his escape. (This Ananias was not the liar.) The Azzim Palace, a fine example of eighteenth-century aristocratic living, Saladin's tomb, the huge Omayyad Mosque, and the* souks *(bazaars) for miles and miles, so colorful. For a finish, the lovely Tequiha Mosque.*—CP

Founded 2,200 years B.C., the desert port of Damascus has been the capital of one government or another for more than 4,000 years (presently of Syria). Legend says, "The world began in Damascus, and the world will end there."

Left: According to the Bible, after his miraculous conversion on the road to Damascus, Paul began to preach in the city, where his enemies caused a warrant to be issued for his arrest. He is said to have escaped by being let down in a *spuris* (basket) from the window in this section of the city's wall.

Right, clockwise from top left: Tiny merchant stalls seem to be everywhere in the city—this one specialized in sandals.

One of the larger *souks* (bazaars), dim and cool, the Long Market stretches a full quarter mile.

People crowd the biblical street called "Straight."

The ever-present military force in the streets of Damascus, the oldest continuously inhabited city in the world.

THE HOLY LAND

MAY 3: *Lunch at Amman in Jordan. On the way, women working on the road in constantly different costume. It seems that each village has its own costume. Camels grazing and many of them. Sheep in huge flocks and beautiful black goats. Bedouin tents scattered on the hillsides. The Allenby bridge over the little, muddy, fast-flowing Jordan. We passed the Mount of Temptation where Satan tempted Christ, also the Inn of the Good Samaritan. We stopped at Jericho, a lovely oasis and then the beautiful Dead Sea, with its Mount Nebo looking at us, where Moses was buried and Joshua took over and brought the Jews back to the Promised Land. All these stories of the Old and the New Testaments, what with two excellent guides, bring back my days in Sunday School when they were such good stories. Being here, they are even more, they are very moving. Jerusalem Friday.*—CP

Above left: Cole and I are having tea at Amman. Called Rabbath Amon in ancient times, it was capital of the fierce and sinful Ammonites of the Old Testament. Note the tea table sitting *in* the fountain before us.

Above: The River Jordan photographed from the Allenby Bridge. The only large flowing river in Palestine, its name comes from the Hebrew *hayyarden*, meaning "flowing downward" or "the descender." The distance it flows between the Sea of Galilee and the Dead Sea is about seventy miles, but the river itself, with its serpentine curves, is about two hundred miles long.

Above right: Eight hundred feet above sea level, Jericho's climate is tropical and the summer heat intense. Springs of water make the locality a lush green oasis in the midst of the dry Jordan rift area. In ancient times it was called the city of palm trees.

Left: Cole studies the rules of deportment at the public beach on the Dead Sea. At thirteen hundred feet below sea level, this is the lowest point on earth.

Below: Marti took these pictures of me at the Syrian border and on the edge of "no-man's-land" at Jerusalem. I knew that Cole had some anxiety about safety traveling in certain parts

of the Holy Land, but I was surprised when I received the following cable prior to our leaving for this trip (February 1, 1956): "I HAVE GOT CERTIFICATE FROM RECTOR ST. BARTHOLOMEW'S SAYING YOU ARE CHRISTIAN THIS WILL SUFFICE. COLE." I suppose he was concerned about the name Feldman, on my passport, being Jewish. At the time I thought it silly; today it seems clairvoyant.

MAY 4: *Jerusalem. Mount of Olives (Ascension), Pater Noster church where Christ gave Lord's prayer to disciples for second time. Garden of Gethsemane, Church of Agony with its rock where Christ prayed, High Priest Caiaphas' house, where he and scribes decided to have Christ crucified and to spare Barabas and where Peter denied Christ. Underneath, prison where Christ was put. Pretorium of the Romans, Ecce Homo gate where Pilate showed Christ to populace. Ecce Homo house where Christ was mocked, scourged, and given crown of thorns. The Via Dolorosa to Church of Holy Sepulchre near Calvary, in a sedan chair.—CP*

Left: I lead the way through the Garden of Gethsemane; Cole follows, looking rather relaxed on wheels.

Right, above and below: The group (Cole and Marti at center) before the Chapel of the Ascension, built on the highest point of the Mount of Olives.

I am standing against one of the seven ancient olive trees that give the Garden of Gethsemane its name— Garden of the Oil Press—from the Hebrew *Gat Shehmanim*.

Below: One of sixty ceramic-tile plaques that line the walls of the entrance and cloister of the Pater Noster church, also located on the Mount of Olives. The plaques each contain the Lord's Prayer in a different language. They were made at the order of the devout Princess de la Tour d'Auvergne, who financed the building in 1874, on the sight of a Crusader church by the same name. The knights believed that Jesus had taught the Lord's Prayer on this spot, though the Bible makes no reference to it.

Right: The main feature of the Garden of Gethsemane is the Church of

the Agony, also called the Church of All Nations because it was financed by contributions from twelve different countries. It was built by Italian architect Antonio Barluzzi in 1924. Remnants of a fourth-century church and a twelfth-century Crusader basilica still remain on the site. The focal point of the church is the "Rock of the Agony," where Jesus is said to have "sweated blood in his anguish." Above and to the right are the onion-shaped cupolas of the Church of Mary Magdalene, built in 1885 by Czar Alexander III in honor of his mother, Maria Alexandrovna.

Cole had long since arranged for Marti and me to have our own car and guide. Our guide this day spoke perfect English in a very dramatic way. His Bible stories were so moving that we were on the verge of tears as we settled ourselves in the car that was taking us to meet Cole for lunch. Suddenly, with hand outstretched from the front seat, holding a small white packet, our guide said, "Would you ladies like a little cocaine?" Startled, we began to laugh. Marti took the packet and looked at me. I said, "Put some on your thumbnail and smell it." She did, and at that moment—as she handed the packet back to our guide—one side of her face became frozen. She had to talk from the side of her mouth as though she had had a shot of Novocain! I cautioned her not to say a word, and, for the first time during the whole trip, Marti *didn't* say a word—I myself said very little. Cole, beaming through the entire lunch, never knew of our adventure in the holiest of holy lands.

Clockwise from left: Every Friday morning the local Franciscan fathers lead a procession along the Via Dolorosa (the Street of Sorrows), visiting the fourteen stations of the cross, the final stages of Christ's Passion. Here, the Franciscans prepare for the procession. They seemed a strange group—accessorizing their monk's robes with very dark sunglasses and the occasional safari hat—some of their expressions look less than pious.

Pilgrims.

Two of the Franciscans; behind them a visiting priest holds his camera and scans the area for a photo opportunity.

A group of the faithful pose with the symbol of their pilgrimage.

The Dome of the Rock (sometimes called the Mosque of Omar) is the most important building on the Temple Mount. Muslims call the thirty-acre rectangle Haram es-Sherif (the Noble Enclosure). The dome we saw in 1956 was the second of three to top this building founded by the Omayyad Caliph, Ab-dal-Malick, in A.D. 691. The first dome was said to have been made of solid gold. This one was made of two hundred tons of lead. The third, installed in 1963, weighing only thirty-five tons, is made of bronze and aluminum. The name is taken from the outcropping of Mount Moriah that the building encloses. It is said to be not only the spot where Abraham prepared to sacrifice his son but also the place where David had his altar, Solomon his temple, and—most romantically—where Buraq, the winged horse with a woman's head and peacock's tail, took Muhammad on his night journey to heaven. (The fountain at left is called El-Kas, The Cup.)

Left: Marti and I looking slightly less than mournful at the Wailing Wall. The holiest sight in Judaism, the wall takes its name from centuries of Jews coming to it to pray and bewail their exile and the destruction of the Temple of Solomon, of which, legend says, only the wall remains. In actuality the wall is of several periods.

Worshipers write their prayers on bits of paper and stick them in the cracks between stones so that they are put directly before their Lord.

Above: This arch takes its name from the words *Ecce Homo* (Behold the Man), which Pilate is said to have uttered below it when he presented Jesus, wearing the crown of thorns, to the crowd after his flagellation.

179

MAY 5: *By chartered DC3 to Ma'an, drive in cars to a police station where horses and donkeys are waiting to take us to Petra. Finally to a great gorge, very high and very narrow where, after a long ride, suddenly everything opened and we were in a vast mysterious city carved out of solid rock and the rock multicolored. It was originally built by the Nabateans, enlarged by the Hellenistic Greeks, and elaborated by the Romans. There is a Roman aqueduct from the beginning of the gorge to the city, and in the city, a big Roman theatre (where did they get the actors?), on every side lovely palaces, temples, and tombs, carved in the solid rock; and even up in the mountains above, all of these becoming more colored by the setting sun. We each had a tent. A good dinner, to which I invited Miss Kirk-Bride, an English archaeologist who is digging here and has found arrows, etc., from the Stone Age. After dinner, Bedouin singers and dancers. Then to Miss Kirk-Bride's big cave where she has been living for months. She has her own stove, a cook, a maid, and many books.* —CP

Characteristically, Cole downplayed the difficulty of the journey to Petra. During the drive, sand came up through the floorboards of the car, nearly suffocating us. At the police station at Elji, it was decided that the trip was too long for Cole to make on a donkey, leaving no choice but to go on horseback. An earlier ride on a horse had resulted in his crippling accident, and, despite his bravado, I know he was terrified to get on a horse now. To make matters worse, his mount was a mare with a young colt that kept trying to run alongside his mother. It was an unforgettable sight to see Cole constantly poking with his cane, which he carried with him always, this little colt to keep him from coming too close to Cole's leg.

Left, above and below: I took these pictures from the air. The first shows the River Jordan as it joins the Dead Sea. The other shows Petra and gives a good idea how isolated it is.

Left, middle: Our group with the chartered plane.

Right, top to bottom: On our way from the police station at Elji, we stopped at Rephidim to examine "Moses' Rock." It is said that here the prophet was ordered to strike his staff, causing barren rock to flow water to refresh the Israelites on their way to Sinai. I am tasting the waters, which flow to this day.

Several years ago, when this picture was published in *Vanity Fair*, the caption referred to Cole as sporting "biblical chic."

Paul, looking rather dashing himself; in the background is a local girl with her washing hung out to dry on a stone wall.

Gerald Harding, then director of Jordan's Department of Antiquities, called Petra "one of the greatest wonders ever wrought by nature or man." And English poet John William Burgon immortalized in verse "this rose-red city half as old as time."

Petra's mighty temples and tombs were carved from pink sandstone cliffs by the mysterious Nabateans more than two thousand years ago. Lost to the world for centuries, today Petra is approached by a solitary canyon entrance—a narrow passage called a *siq*, which makes a mile-long slash in the mountains of biblical Edom.

Left: At the end of the *siq* one can see a sliver of El-Khazne. Like all the monuments at Petra, what appear to be buildings are not buildings at all. They are architectural spaces carved directly into living rock. From a distance the overall impression is one of rose red; close up, the stone is streaked with a rainbow of pastel colors, described by Rose Macauley as resembling "the shifting hues of watered silk."

Right: El-Khazne is also called the Pharaoh's Treasury because Arab shepherds believed that only the builders of the Great Pyramids could have been responsible for such an edifice. The urn at the top has been battered away by the bullets of local Bedouins, who even in modern times believe that a lucky shot will release a shower of gold—the pharaoh's treasure hidden within.

At its height the Roman settlement here covered more than two miles of this hidden valley. The only remaining inhabitants are a few Bedouins who live mostly from money earned by working as guides and bearers for visitors. The children spend whatever comes their way on European cigarettes as happily as if on a trip to the candy store.

In the 1950s it became a craze among Israeli teenagers to visit Petra—a sort of rite of passage—braving the Jordanian patrols that eventually killed three of them. A pop song, "El Hasela Ha'adom" ("To the Red Rock"), went straight to the top of the Israeli hit parade.

Left: Marti and Cole enjoying the Bedouin music together.

Right, above and below: A group of Bedouin men by the campfire.

This handsome Bedouin, who looked just like Tyrone Power, was happy to pose for me. All of a sudden he proceeded to slap his thigh as he said to me in perfect English, "Sleep." I responded, "It's only 9:30"—not knowing if he was making a pass or if he really wanted to sleep.

This page, clockwise from top left: Waking up at 6:30 A.M.—Ugh!—Cole never traveled without his coffee cup, and I never traveled without my "Frownie."

The facilities.

Marti waking up with a yawn. We both had put on every-

thing we could find to sleep in; the nights were freezing cold.

Right: Properly dressed in his navy blue suit, Paul serves Cole breakfast before his tent. Cole's own breakfast service was another of the contents of all that luggage; it traveled with him everywhere.

Clockwise from left: With guides, Marti and I make our way up to the highest place in Petra.

The oldest of the caves are the plainest; this is the entrance to the one occupied by Miss Kirk-Bride. Another of the caves contained a large guest book for visitors. When Cole came back to our tent after signing his name in the book, he said to me, "You will never believe the last names signed in that book: They were Dorothy and Lillian Gish!"—those famous sisters who loved to travel.

Almost as old as the caves are the "obelisk" tombs, such as this one.

The stepped decoration on this tomb is typical of the Nabatean contribution to Petra's evolving architecture.

The enormous twenty-six-foot doorway to El Deir.

Also called the monastery, El Deir is the largest and least accessible monument at Petra. More or less a copy of the treasury, it is slightly larger.

MAY 6: *Sunday. After lunch, back to Jerusalem and on the way, constant evidences of the Arab Legion, of whom many are British, the whole outfit formed and still trained by the British. They wear British uniforms, very smart, but Arab headdresses (the* caipha *or scarf and the* egal *or double cord to keep the* caipha *on). We all wore these headdresses, beginning with our ride to Petra. They are most practical in the desert as they can be adjusted in any number of ways to protect one against the wind, cold, heat, dust, and flies.*

MAY 7: *Bethlehem and the Church of the Nativity. The extraordinary thing about this "Holy Land" is not the spots, as most of the spots are mere conjecture. The moving part of it all is the Christians who have come from the entire world to worship.* —CP

I am especially proud of these two pictures taken at the Church of the Nativity in Bethlehem. Originally built in A.D. 326 by Constantine and rebuilt in the sixth century by Justinian on the sight of the Emperor Hadrian's Grove of Adonis, the church is now shared by three Christian denominations—Roman Catholic, Greek Orthodox, and Armenian. Below the central Altar of the Nativity is the Grotto of the Nativity. Lit only by lamplight, the grotto was very dark, and I was without a flash. I placed my Rolleiflex on a ledge and set it for a full minute's exposure. I was amazed that I got anything at all, but here they are. The silver star on the floor, dated 1717, is inscribed, *"Hic de Virgine Maria Jesus Christus natus est"* ("Here Jesus Christ was born of the Virgin Mary").

MAY 8: *Plane to Beirut. Most of the plane occupied by very old Greek Orthodox peasants returning to their homes in Australia after having visited Jerusalem to pray. Two of them could barely walk. They all must have spent their life savings for this pilgrimage.*
MAY 9: *Arrive Istanbul and Horrible Hilton. Outrageous invasion of press and photographers.*
MAY 10: *St. Sophia, Blue Mosque, Suleiman [Süleyman I] Mosque, former sultans' palace, to see jewels (fabulous and hideous).*
MAY 11: *A drive to the Black Sea along the Bosphorus. One villa after another, each one more repulsive than the other, but the Bosphorus beautiful, looking very much like the Hudson. Back to the palace of the sultans, to see a huge collection of porcelain, most of it very valuable and very ugly. To the seven walls, to see the prison where people's heads were cut off and dropped in a hole to float or sink in the Sea of Marmora.*—CP

Cole wanted to avoid the press as much as possible. He turned against the Hilton hotel in Istanbul because hotel officials allowed them in—all the way in—the press actually walked straight in and found Cole in his bathtub. He was furious. The hotel did make the newspeople turn over the negatives, which Cole destroyed, but he didn't calm down.

Left: Built in only seven years (1609–16), the Mosque of Ahmet I is better known as the Blue Mosque because of the color of the glazed tiles that cover its interior walls. Of all mosques only this one has six minarets.

Right: A man at prayer before one of the Blue Mosque's 260 windows.

MAY 12: *Athens, bless it, and the charming Grande-Bretagne.*
MAY 13: *Dined with Spiros Harocopos in his beautiful apartment, the walls lined with fine Byzantine ikons. Among the guests, Paxinou, the actress.*
MAY 15: *Tuesday. Lunch aboard Eros; same charming crew. First stop, Hydra, a peaceful island. Visited late Byzantine church with lovely ikons.*
MAY 16: *Parso, famous for marble quarries. Visited eleventh-century church, Byzantine, full of charming, simple carvings on varied marbles. At sunset, passed Naxos.*
MAY 17: *Cos (or Kos). The fortress of the Crusaders, facing the coast of Turkey, the huge plane tree under which Hippocrates is supposed to have first taught hygiene and curing (don't believe it). Hippocrates was born in Cos; the Asclepieion, the first spa in history, supposedly founded by Hippocrates, recently very restored by the Greek government.*

In the evening, after a beautiful sail, arrived Patmos and its enchanting harbor.—CP

Left, above and below: The great Greek actress Katina Paxinou with her husband, Alex Minotis; together they established the celebrated Royal Theater of Athens. One of the most famous actresses in Greece, she gained world fame when she won the Oscar as best supporting actress in the 1943 film *For Whom the Bell Tolls.*

About four miles east of Athens is the suburb of Kaisariani and its monastery, with the Church of Panagia Kaisariani set among cypress, pine, and plane trees. The name comes from a nearby ancient healing spring called Kyllu Pera and later Kaisariani Pigi (Imperial Spring), after Hadrian caused an aqueduct to be built to carry water to the people of Athens. The present church was built about A.D. 1000 on the site of an earlier fifth-century Christian church. The bell tower is a seventeenth-century addition.

Below: The island of Cos has been well populated since Neolithic times. Among the ancients it was famous as the first cult site of Asklepios, the god of healing. Cole was right about the tree—Hippocrates taught on Cos in

the fifth century B.C.—scientists say that it may be the oldest plane tree in Europe, but it is only about five hundred years old. As you can see, one of its largest boughs was supported by a marble column when we were there. Today the girth of the trunk has increased to forty feet and the huge boughs are supported by a less romantic metal scaffold.

Friday. Patmos. We were taken in a truck by a terrifying road to a mountaintop to the Monastery of St. John the Divine, founded in the eleventh century. An old monk suddenly spoke to me in good English. He had been born on Patmos, went to the U.S.A., hated the bustle so much that he had come back here and had become a monk in a monastery "to find God and Eternal Peace." On the way down, to St. John's cave, where he lived after having been exiled from Rome by Domitian and where he wrote the Revelation.—CP

The Monastery of St. John the Divine crowns the mountaintop at Chora, on the island of Patmos. It was founded in 1088 by the powerful Abbot Christodoulos from Asia Minor. Among the monastery's many treasures are beautiful icons, three thousand rare books, nearly a thousand manuscripts dating from the sixth to nineteenth century, and ship pendants made of diamonds and emeralds donated by Catherine the Great.

Within weeks after our visit, the monastery was heavily damaged by an earthquake. Although many walls are now given support by wooden beams, a more positive result of this damage was the discovery, beneath the seventeenth-century frescoes, of paintings executed five hundred years earlier.

A fifteen-minute walk from Chora, below the Monastery of the Apocalypse, is the Cave of St. Anne, or St. John, that Cole refers to. The cave has been converted into a church, its massive ceiling—legend says—"split in three by the voice of God."

Left: Marti and I stand with our host.
Right: Cole with a member of the *Eros* crew on the truck ride up the mountain.

198

MAY 19: *Samos. A drive to vast ruin of Temple of Hera, facing nearby coast of Turkey. Temple made of blue Samion marble, one huge column left standing.*

In the evening, we arrive Chios, a sheltered harbor. Most of our crew comes from Chios. The captain's wife and two daughters, our chief steward, Niko's wife, daughter, and mother come aboard. These women are all beautiful, still retaining the widely separated eyes, the fine noses, and the small mouths of the classic Greek sculptures. We all drink and have hors d'oeuvres together, smiling and not being able to exchange one word.

MAY 20: *By car and then by donkey to Nea Moni (New Monastery), eleventh century, to see fine Byzantine mosaics comparable to those of Osias Lukas and Daphne. Our departure from monastery (now a nunnery) delayed by Mother Superior who gave us a fig liqueur and* loukoum *made of rose petals. Both great. Lunch in a lovely spot under big plane trees. Later, dinner by the sea, and a terrible orchestra, but always top food.*

All these people on the islands are alike in their simplicity, their dignity, and their happiness.

MAY 21: *Lesbos (Mytilene). A drive through mountainous but very fertile country to Ayassos, where ugly church contains beautiful small ikons, some of them resembling Persian miniatures.*—CP

Left, top: Marti and me on Samos. I was much more interested in the little stone house in the background than the Temple of Hera, and thought seriously about buying it.

Left, bottom: Marti took this picture of me, looking rather like Captain Ahab, trying desperately to control the wheel against the forces of Neptune. Of course the boat was sitting perfectly still—with a little time to kill before going ashore, we were just having fun.

Left, middle, and at right: Niko with his wife (left) and daughter.

Cole, our guide, Niko, Marti, and Bob.

201

Above and below: Marti and I discovered this little waterfront café, which was full of sailors and seemed nothing special, until one of the musicians got up and began to dance. Suddenly he picked up one of the rather solidly built tables (glasses, beer bottles, and all) in his teeth and continued to dance around the room. Funny and fantastic!

Right: The beautiful harbor at Chios.

May 22: *Thasos (looking like the mountains of New Hampshire). We had a private bus to see ruins of 450 B.C. city and the museum containing a strange archaic statue of Apollo, practically Egyptian. Also beautiful horses' heads and a sculpture of Venus without her upper half riding a delightful dolphin. Thasos honey was brought aboard, the most powerful honey in Greece. Many bees on deck though we were moored far from the shore. Slightly to the north, the coast of Macedonia.*—CP

Left, clockwise from top left: Upon our arrival at Thasos, the island people presented Marti and me with flowers. They grow wild all over the island and are of course important to the honey production there. Cole arranged to have some of the honey sent to New York—it was great.

Bob and I stroll on a typical Thasos street.

Bob and Marti with our private bus.

Right, clockwise from left: The Apollo Cole mentioned is called Apollo Kriophoros and is eleven feet tall. Begun in the sixth century B.C., the strange geometric look is due to its never having been finished.

One of the beautiful horse's heads.

The contrast between the rigid Apollo and this graceful head gives an indication of the many periods of sculpture (from about 700 B.C. through Roman times) displayed in this small but fine museum.

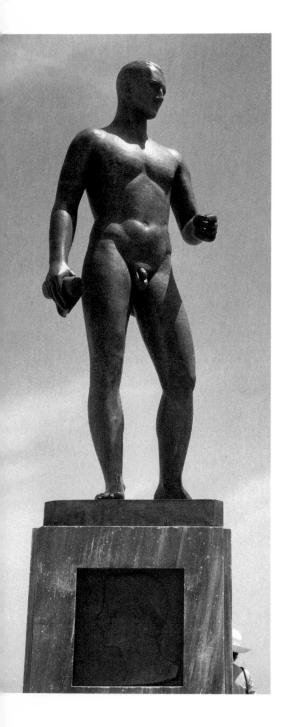

MAY 23: Mt. Athos. *We skirted the southern and the western coasts all morning looking through binoculars at numerous monasteries, some on the shore, others high on the mountainside. These monasteries are so big they look like villages; some of them are occupied by Greek monks, others by Bulgarian, Russian, or Serbian monks. Many monks, however, prefer to live in groups of only two or three while the most ascetic of all live completely alone in caves or eagles' nests.*

After lunch we first visited Dochiarion monastery near the shore. The interior of the church is entirely painted in the eleventh-century Byzantine style, though done in the sixteenth century. Beautiful. We met several monks, all old except one young man named Innocent who, in spite of his mustache and beard and long hair, looked like Audrey Hepburn.

Farther along the coast, Monastery of Dionysiou high on a cliff. Service was going on in the dusk of the church here, the monks all sitting in choir stalls around the edges and those participating in the service wearing black veils. Each monk seemed to be chanting a different chant, the whole effect nearly terrifying. After service, we were taken into a small sitting room to be given anisette, loukoum, *and coffee, while an old monk who had spent eight years in the U.S.A. talked to us in fluent broken English about Atlanta, Georgia; Houston "good town," Texas; New York City ("too cold"); Chicago ("too cold"), and Los Angeles ("warm"). What he liked best in the U.S.A. was the Automat.*

We didn't attempt to go to the monastery of Grand Lavra, though to get there one no longer has to be lifted up to it in a basket as there is a new steep road. But to get to the road one must go for many hours, mule-back.

The monasteries of Mt. Athos used to have 40,000 monks. Now there are only 2,000, and very few young men want to come here and become monks. The ones who are here do no good for the world. This has always been true. They have merely retired from life. The ones I met today seemed to be happy but nearly infantile. They all pray at least eight hours a day. Some in the less strict monasteries till small plots of land, which they own. Others sit around and live on the income of the monasteries into which they have retired, the income derived from properties the monasteries own on many nearby islands and lands. It is a strange experience to have been here, and fascinating, but it reeks of rot. (Look up Meteora monasteries of Thessaly.)

MAY 24: Thursday. Skiros (Northern Sporades). *Drove to town of Skiros, highly picturesque, rather like Mykonos but much higher and more dramatic. Saw memorial statue to Rupert Brooke with inscription, "To Rupert Brooke and Immortal Poetry." In museum, pottery of Cretan and Mycenaean civilizations mostly discovered by University of California archaeologist Dorothy Hanson.*—CP

Cole's visit to Mount Athos made a deep impression on him. Unfortunately, I was not able to go with him that day because the monks do not allow female visitors. "We are not antiwomen," claimed a spokesman for the monks, "but we keep them out to avoid scandals and disgrace."

Left: Rupert Brooke died here in 1915, at the age of twenty-eight, on his way to fight in the Dardanelles. This memorial, on Mount Kokhilas, overlooks Tris Boúkes Bay far below, where he is buried. On clear days Mount Athos can be seen in the distance across the water.

Right: The town of Skiros, Mykonos in the mountains.

MAY 25: *Skopelos (near Skiros), another peaceful isle. We didn't land. At sunset, Skiathos, a port full of fishing boats and no automobiles. When the Germans had to leave this port at the end of World War II, they bombed the town and set it afire. It has been charmingly rebuilt.*

MAY 26: *Saturday. Cruised to another part of Skiathos and moored off a lovely sandy beach backed by huge pines. Then on to the gulf that separates northern Greece from Euboea. On our right we saw Mt. Olympus and, farther south, the mountain beyond, which is the Pass of Thermopylae. In the evening we laid anchor at Chalkis. To the right is Tanagra.*

MAY 27: *Sunday. Chalkis, farther on. From the bay here, the Greek fleet sailed for the Trojan War. Drove first to museum to see fine archaic sculptures from Eretria, then to Eretria, destroyed by Persians in 490 B.C. A few foundations left.*

MAY 28: *Proceeded toward Petali. On our right, the plain of Marathon, Mt. Pentelikon, and, farther still, Mt. Hymettus. Anchored off Petali, island owned by Embericos family. In the evening, a completely calm sea, the stars nearly on our heads, and silence.*

MAY 29: *Had breakfast, as usual, on deck. Arrived at Piraeus and the beautiful cruise is over. On the way to the Grande-Bretagne, we stopped to see the Mycenaean gold, which is once more exposed at the museum.*

In the evening to the Benaki Museum, which was specially opened for us, after hours, to see fascinating Greek regional costume and jewelry, plus a fine collection of ikons. —CP

Cole didn't say good-bye that May in Athens. The day after our return he left this note *(near right)* for me at our hotel.

Marti and I went on to Rome to do some shopping, after which she went to London and I returned to California.

That summer through the end of the year, Cole stayed in California and worked on the score for *Les Girls,* his new film project for MGM. He also wrote additional songs for the film version of *Silk Stockings.*

In October *High Society* opened and proved my point—"True Love" became the most played song of the year. When it lost the Oscar to "Que Sera, Sera," George Eells—who had watched the telecast with him—reported Cole's reaction: "The smile never left Cole's face as he picked up the telephone and asked for Western Union. To (Stanley) Musgrove (Cole's public relations man) he sent the following message: "WHATEVER WILL BE, WILL BE, DEAR STANLEY. COLE."

Left: Marti, with the captain and crew, back at Pireaus.
Far right: On the *Eros,* near the end of our voyage.

May 30, th 5-6.

HOTEL GRANDE-BRETAGNE
"LE PETIT PALAIS"

ATHÉNES
GRÈCE

TELEGRAMME : HOTBRITAN
TELEPHONE : 30.251
16 LIGNES

Dear Jean —
        Robert has to stand
by in Rome to find out
when he must hit Holly-
wood & I'm going along
for the ride.
        So goodbye, have
fun & my love to you
both.

                Cole.

FRIENDSHIP

May 5, 1945

Dear Jeannie & Charlie—
What a beautiful welcome! Really, that party for me was
a triumph of thoughtfulness. And though I spent all my time
laughing, I kept thinking of the two of you & your great
friendship & I wanted to cry.

Your devoted Cole

POSTCARD

April 30 [1957]

The rain in Italy stays mainly in Bologna
Love

Cole.

FROM: COLE PORTER

September 7, 1957

Dear Jean:
    I enclose a copy of the order from the people who
will ship you the two Linda Porter rose bushes. They
inform me that they will probably be shipped in
December.
    I miss you awfully and I wish you would come
back quick. Nice dinners continue rather often. For
the first time I went to the Buddy Adlers for dinner. It
was extraordinary—such a beautiful house and food
for the Gods. Perhaps the dinner wasn't big enough
for you—there were only nineteen—but, of course,
I am a simple boy from Indiana who likes quiet
evenings.

Lots of love—

Cole

CP:te

416 N. Rockingham Avenue
Los Angeles 49
California

Above: Posing in my garden with one of
the "Linda Porter" rose bushes Cole had sent me.
Right: Two people who helped Cole keep his world in order:
Paul Sylvain at Cape Sounion, 1955, and Madeline P. Smith, Cole's
New York secretary for twenty-four years—she always referred
to him as "the little boss."

aFTER THE 1956 TRIP Cole discussed traveling with me only once. In late November he called to ask if I could stop by his apartment at the Waldorf Towers that afternoon at 2:00 P.M. —an unusual hour I thought.

He was in his famous "sitting room–library," which Billy Baldwin had designed for him while we were away the previous year. He told me that he was planning to go to Jamaica; before I could say anything—he quickly added, "I'll need a hostess." Though I was puzzled, I said, "O.K., here I am." Then, slowly and distinctly he said, "But I want to make it legal." Surprised, I laughed and said, "O.K., it's legal." Looking at my watch, I made an excuse about being late for an appointment. Walking me through the hallway, he stopped and said, "Just a moment, I want you to meet someone."

A tall, good-looking man walked out of Cole's office. "Jean, I want you to meet Robert Montgomery, my lawyer." We shook hands politely and then I said that I was late and had to run, "good-bye."

That was the first and last time that I ever saw Mr. Montgomery —to this day I'm not sure what was on Cole's mind when he said he wanted to make it legal. If not marriage, what? It was never mentioned again. At the time I didn't quite know why I couldn't even consider marriage to Cole. Over the years I have come to realize that whereas I always wanted to "be Linda Porter," I wasn't and could never have been Linda. Anything less would not have suited him.

Just before Linda died she had said to Cole, "I hate being forgotten and I'm not important enough. . . . If only I were [famous], so that a flower or something could be named for me." That same day he began arrangements that would result, on August 28, 1954, in the announcement of the granting of a patent on the "Linda Porter Rose." The strain was achieved by the crossing of two varieties of tea roses, which created an unusually fragrant soft pink bloom that when fully opened measured four-and-one-half-to-six inches.

In April of 1957 Cole flew to Italy; aside from Paul, his only traveling companion was Bob Bray. While there, and in France, he made his last visits to Venice and Paris. He saw Dickie Fellowes-Gordon again, Henry May (looking very ill), Christos Bellos, and his old friend Bernard Berenson, who talked almost exclusively of Linda. When Paul developed a back problem, the trip was cut short and Cole returned to New York on May 14.

From late 1957 until his death, Cole would spend many weeks, sometimes months, in hospitals—mostly the Harkness Pavilion. Bentley, his chauffeur, would pick me up at my apartment on East Seventy-seventh Street—always at 5:30—and get me to the hospital exactly at 6:10, when Cole received visitors. Seated in a wheelchair in a little gallery, (a space reserved for visitors, not in his room), Cole always opened his arms wide and said, "Tell me your news!" He would have his drink and visitors had a choice of a drink or tea. It was all done in the perfect Porter manner—served by his valets.

At times when Cole was not in the hospital, I often dined with him at his apartment, or if he felt up to it, we had lunch or dinner at La Côte Basque, which was new and very popular at the time. There were also many weekends at Williamstown.

On July 21, 1959, Paul Sylvain—"The Great Paul"—died. To my mind, Paul was the greatest friend, in the best sense of the word, of all Cole's friends—and in the last years of his life, Cole himself realized that it was Paul's constant concern that had kept him going for so long. Upon Paul's death, Cole immediately set up a $75,000 trust fund for Paul's two small daughters, Faith and Hope.

On May 12, 1964, I had dinner alone with Cole. I do not remember much of what was said. I only remember him picking at his food with half-closed eyes. I remember this because it had been

---

FROM: COLE PORTER

August 8, 1959

Dearest Jean:
    I have just come back from the hospital, where I had intestinal trouble, and found two postcards from you.
    Paul died on July 21st. It had to be but I shall never cease to miss him. Wasn't he wonderful?
        Love—

Cole

CP:te

416 N. Rockingham Avenue
Los Angeles 49
California

FROM: COLE PORTER

THE TOWERS
THE WALDORF-ASTORIA
NEW YORK

June 29, 1964

Dearest Jean:—
    Thank you so much for your note. I hope you will come to the West Coast during the summer.
        Love,

Cole

CP:ms

Dear Mrs. H:—
    He is back now in 33-A—but weak. He really plans on going to Calif. this Saturday.

        Best,
        M.P.S.

A Reminder

Cole Porter

expects you for *Dinner*

on *Tuesday, May 12ᵗʰ*

at *8³⁰* o'clock

Waldorf Towers
Apt. 33-A

Informal

Cole Porter with his wife, the former Linda Lee Thomas in 1954, the year she died. They were married 25 years.

FROM: COLE PORTER

July 12, 1964

Dearest Jean:

Your letter of July 6th, from London, arrived and made me very happy. I do hope you will come to California later and, if possible, with Michael.

Lots of Love.

Cole

CP:te

this way for so long. You simply did not exist for him at times like this. After dinner we went back to his sitting room–library, and it was here that I told Cole that I was leaving for Europe in a few days. He asked, "No California this year?" I explained that Charlie had the house that summer and that I would not be going west. Then he said, "I'll miss you, Jeannie," and closed his eyes—he seemed to be in a deep sleep. I slipped out of the room. How could I know that this was the last time that I would see Cole?

By this time I was having problems of my own—a broken friendship—the pain of losing when I thought I was loved. Cole knew this kind of pain, and in his own way, he told us so in many of his songs. On June 6 I left for London for, my diary says, "thirty-five terrible days." Shortly after I left, Cole was hospitalized again with a variety of maladies.

We continued to correspond. A short note with addendum by Cole's secretary, Madeline P. Smith, informed me that Cole would be leaving for California in early July.

On July 12 I received what would be my last note from Cole, saying that he hoped he would see Michael Pearman and me in California "later."

Having spent August and most of September traveling in Italy and Switzerland, I returned to London for my birthday on October 13. It was here, on the 16th, that Tony Santoro brought me a newspaper and asked, "Is this your friend Cole Porter?" The headline read, "Cole Porter dead in Santa Monica, California."

After all those endearing and funny telegrams—"what a great day"—my heart broke a little.

Over the years there have been comments about Cole dying alone as though he were some pathetic forgotten figure. The fact is, at his own request no one really knew he was even in the hospital again. When Cole entered St. John's Hospital in Santa Monica in mid-October, only his friend the agent Bob Raison knew, and Cole requested that his dinner engagements for the next week be rescheduled—telling no one why. These engagements included Vivien Leigh, Merle Oberon, Julie Andrews, Natalie Schafer, and George Cukor—hardly the calendar of a lonely, forgotten man. The last week, Cole was visited daily by Bob Raison and Stanley Musgrove and attended by his valets Eric and Henry until he died on October 15.

I am happy to share some of my recollections of over thirty years of friendship with Cole Porter. Since nature plays such naughty tricks on all of us, it's quite possible that within a couple of years you might ask me to tell you about Cole, and I could say—"COLE WHO?"

We could go on and on about friendship—but let's turn to the light side of
Cole Porter and end this book not in tears but in laughter. Both Cole
and Linda offered me friendship, and it lasted their lifetimes. In
his own flip way with words, Cole said it all in a comedy song
written for Ethel Merman and Bert Lahr in the 1939 show
Du Barry Was a Lady:

FRIENDSHIP

REFRAIN 1

He: *If you're ever in a jam, here I am.*
She: *If you ever need a pal, I'm your gal.*
He: *If you ever feel so happy you land in jail,*
I'm your bail.
Both: *It's friendship, friendship,*
Just a perfect blendship,
When other friendships have been forgot,
Ours will still be hot.
Lahdle—ahdle—ahdle—dig, dig, dig.

REFRAIN 2

She: *If you ever lose your way, come to May.*
He: *If you ever make a flop, call on Pop.*
She: *If you ever take a boat and get lost at sea,*
Write to me.
Both: *It's friendship, friendship,*
Just a perfect blendship.
When other friendships have been forgit,
Ours will still be it.
Lahdle—ahdle—ahdle—chuck, chuck, chuck.

REFRAIN 3

He: *If you're ever down a well, ring my bell.*
She: *If you ever catch on fire, send a wire.*
He: *If you ever loose your teeth and you're out to dine,*
Borrow mine.
Both: *It's friendship, friendship,*
Just a perfect blendship,
When other friendships have ceased to jell
Ours will still be swell.
Lahdle—ahdle—ahdle—hep, hep, hep.

REFRAIN 4

She: *If they ever black your eyes, put me wise.*
He: *If they ever cook your goose, turn me loose.*

She: *If they ever put a bullet to your brr-ain,*
I'll complain.
Both: *It's friendship, friendship,*
Just a perfect blendship.
When other friendships go up in smoke
Ours will still be oke.
Lahdle—ahdle—ahdle—chuck, chuck, chuck.
Gong, gong, gong,
Cluck, cluck, cluck,
Woof, woof, woof,
Peck, peck, peck,
Put, put, put,
Hip, hip, hip.
Quack, quack, quack,
Tweet, tweet, tweet,
Push, push, push,
Give, give, give.

REFRAIN 5

He: *If you ever lose your mind, I'll be kind.*
She: *If you ever lose your shirt, I'll be hurt.*
He: *If you're ever in a mill and get sawed in half,*
I won't laugh.
Both: *It's friendship, friendship,*
Just a perfect blendship.
When other friendships have been forgate,
Ours will still be great.
Lahdle—ahdle—ahdle—goof, goof, goof.

REFRAIN 6

She: *If they ever hang you, pard, send a card.*
He: *If you ever cut your throat, write a note.*
She: *If they ever make a cannibal stew of you,*
Invite me too.
Both: *It's friendship, friendship,*
Just a perfect blendship.
When other friendships are up the crick,
Ours will still be slick.
Lahdle—ahdle—ahdle—zip, zip, zip.

Left, top to bottom: *Whenever one had an engagement*
with Cole, a formal reminder was forthcoming — this was the
last I would receive.
This clipping appeared in newspapers in 1960 — the picture was
taken in Athens (1956) — with a caption identifying me as Linda.
My last note from Cole.

INDEX

Love from
one of your
fiancées,
Cole

Dear Jeannie —

COLE PORTER

These are
flowers. Love Cole

A happy
birthday
COLE PORTER
Sweet & wonderful
Jeannie. Your
Cole

My pet!
from
COLE PORTER
Cole

A merry Christmas
for a good girl
COLE PORTER
with affection from
her ole pappy —
Cole

Goodbye
& love
Cole